WALSH

a
play
by
Sharon
Pollock

copyright © 1973 Sharon Pollock

published with assistance from the Canada Council

Talonbooks
201 1019 East Cordova
Vancouver
British Columbia V6A 1M8
Canada

This book was typeset and designed by Beverly Matsu
for Talonbooks.

This script is the Stratford, Ontario version of the play.

Third printing: January 1976

Talonplays are edited by Peter Hay.

ISBN 0-88922-053-0

Walsh was first performed at Theatre Calgary in Calgary, Alberta, on November 7, 1973, with the following cast:

Harry, a wagon master	Frank J. Adamson
Clarence, a new recruit to the NWMP	Hardee T. Lineham
Louis, a Metis scout	Jean Archambault
Walsh, a superintendent of the NWMP in charge of Fort Walsh	Michael Fletcher
Mrs. Anderson, a settler	Margaret Barton
Crow Eagle, a Cree	Stephen Russell
McCutcheon, a Sergeant in the NWMP	Ron Chudley
Gall, a chief of the Hunkpapa Sioux	Denis Lacroix
Sitting Bull, a chief of the Hunkpapa Sioux	August Schellenberg
White Dog, an Assiniboin	Nolan Jennings
Crowfoot, son of Sitting Bull	Frank Turningrobe Jr.
Colonel MacLeod, Commissioner of the NWMP	Hutchison Shandro

Directed by Harold G. Baldridge
Settings & Lights by Richard Roberts
Costumes by Jane Grose
Production Manager   Allan Sheppard
Stage Manager   Bartley Bard

Walsh was also performed at the Third Stage in Stratford, Ontario, on July 24, 1974, with the following cast:

Harry, a wagon master	J. Kenneth Campbell
Clarence, a new recruit to the NWMP	John Stewart
Louis, a Metis scout	Jonathan Welsh
Walsh, a superintendent of the NWMP in charge of Fort Walsh	Michael Ball
Mrs. Anderson, a settler	Donna Farron
Crow Eagle, a Cree	Terry Judd
McCutcheon, a Sergeant in the NWMP	David Hemblen
Gall, a chief of the Hunkpapa Sioux	John Bayliss
Sitting Bull, a chief of the Hunkpapa Sioux	Derek Ralston
White Dog, an Assiniboin	Terry Judd
Crowfoot, son of Sitting Bull	Tim Jones
Colonel MacLeod, Commissioner of the NWMP	John Bayliss
Pretty Plume, wife of Sitting Bull	Donna Farron
Mary, wife of Major Walsh	Donna Farron

Directed by John Wood
Designed by John Ferguson
Music and Sound by Alan Laing
Technical Engineering by Charles Richmond

Prologue

*The characters in the Prologue become the characters
in the play proper. McCUTCHEON plays IAN, the
bartender. SITTING BULL is the PROSPECTOR,
CROW EAGLE is BILLY, the harmonica player in
the saloon. LOUIS and MacLEOD are a couple of
poker players. CROWFOOT is JOEIE, the newspaper
boy. JENNIE is MRS. ANDERSON. WALSH and
HARRY play themselves. WALSH is in civvies,
impeccably dressed, in contrast to the other characters
who look dirty and disreputable. The atmosphere in
the Prologue is smoky, as if the scene were lit by a
coal-oil lamp with a dirty chimney.*

*The scene is from WALSH's point of view, and the
freezes are momentary arrests in the action and are
broken by the character's speech or action following.
The impression given is similar to that experienced
when one is drunk or under great mental stress.
CLARENCE stands outside the Prologue scene never*

taking his eyes off WALSH. He has on his red tunic, and exits only in WALSH's mind. He is not part of that Prologue scene and his scream is heard only by WALSH.

There is no break in staging between the Prologue and Act 1.

The sound of the wind, a mournful sound. In a very dim light the characters suddenly appear on the periphery of the playing area. WALSH is not among them. They freeze there for a moment, and then quickly and silently, like ghosts, take their positions on stage, with the exception of HARRY, JOEIE, and CLARENCE, who remain in the shadows. The characters freeze on stage, all facing WALSH's entrance. There is an increase in the howl of the wind, and WALSH appears in a spot of light somewhat brighter than the general dim lighting. The wind fades as WALSH enters, walking very slowly and carefully, as if the tiniest bit drunk. As he enters, JENNIE pulls out a chair at the table, and IAN pours a drink into the glass on the table. The PROSPECTOR is blocking WALSH's way, and WALSH stops. The PROSPEC-TOR steps aside and WALSH continues towards table as all watch him. WALSH stops at chair, looks out at CLARENCE, and turns the chair so he no longer faces CLARENCE. WALSH sits. There is a momentary freeze, then WALSH reaches for his drink breaking the freeze. BILLY begins playing the harmonica, JENNIE begins to sing, and to move amongst the characters tipping a hat here, and rubbing an arm there as she passes. The characters come alive and the light brightens a bit so that WALSH's spot is gone, although the light is still not full.

JENNIE: *singing*

> George Carmack on Bonanza Creek went out to look
> for gold,
> I wonder why, I wonder why.
> Old-timers said it was no use, the water was too cold.
> I wonder why, I wonder why.

PROSPECTOR:
Another verse, Jennie!

JENNIE:
Is there somethin' else you'd have me do, Mr. Walsh?

WALSH:
Do you know . . . "Break the News to Mother"?

JENNIE:
There's not much I don't know — how the hell did
you think I ended up in Dawson?

Laughs and guffaws from the boys.

WALSH:
I always liked "Break the News to Mother".

JENNIE: *sings*

> I wonder why, I wonder why.

HARRY: *enters from shadows*
Jeeeesus Chriiiist! It's colder than a witch's diddy.

*They all turn to look at him with the exception of
WALSH.*

How about some eats here.

JENNIE:
Girls upstairs to the left, a drink we can give you
here.

BILLY:
> But you can't buy what there ain't none of . . .

PROSPECTOR:
> Which is grub.

A momentary freeze which affects everyone, but WALSH who looks at HARRY.

JENNIE: *sings with BILLY playing harmonica*

> They said that he might search that creek until the world did end,
> But not enough of gold he'd find a postage stamp to send —

JENNIE stops singing abruptly as HARRY pulls out his poke. A momentary freeze by all but WALSH, broken by hoarse whispers.

BILLY:
> Better put away that poke, mister.

PROSPECTOR:
> We got a grafter in the room   *indicating WALSH*
> Ain't you noticed?

JENNIE:
> He'd as soon take 10% of the top of that as look at you.

WALSH: *raises his glass to them*
> Gentlemen, and sweet Jennie.

BILLY: *low*
> To hell with Mr. Walsh.

A momentary freeze as they watch WALSH drink. The freeze is broken by WALSH putting down his glass. IAN moves to fill it. BILLY begins playing "Garryowen" on the harmonica.

HARRY:
Where'd you hear that song? You a Yankee fella?
You a cavalry man?

BILLY:
Don't have to be a cavalry man to know a song, mister.
resumes playing

JENNIE:
Here's a lady done a lot of ridin' and she don't know
that song.

PROSPECTOR:
"Garryowen".

*WALSH knocks over his drink. A momentary freeze
as they look at WALSH and he stares at his spilt
drink.*

JENNIE:
Ah Mr. Walsh, you've spilt your drink. A drink for
Mr. Walsh.

IAN rights the glass, and pours a drink.

BILLY:
To hell with Mr. Walsh. *He resumes playing and
"Garryowen" builds with the sound of a military
band creeping in and growing in volume.*

HARRY:
"Garryowen". Marching song of the 7th Cavalry,
Custer's outfit.

JENNIE:
Who's that?

HARRY:
A long hair killed with his long knives at the Greasy
Grass.

JENNIE:
> We speak English here, mister.

> *"Garryowen" stops abruptly. WALSH bangs down his glass. A freeze as he looks around slowly and speaks clearly, carefully, announcing it, giving the impression once again of being perhaps drunk, but completely under control.*

WALSH:
> General George Armstrong Custer . . . killed with 261 men of the 7th Cavalry of the United States Army . . . at the Little Big Horn, Montana, June 25th, 1876. *A pause. Freeze is broken as he picks up his drink.*

> *BILLY begins a ragtime tune on the harmonica, the lights brighten. The characters resume.*

HARRY:
> Who's your grafter?

IAN:
> That's Major Walsh — but he's not with the Force — he's Commissioner of the Yukon now.

JENNIE:
> Did you see me front? Not a bit of snow to the street. Walsh may not be with the Force but he gets a good day's work out of 'em. *laughs* I must be the only whore house in the north whose front is shovelled clear by the North West Mounted on the orders of the Comissioner of the Yukon. *They look at WALSH.* He knows what those boys are good for.

JOEIE: *moving out of the shadows*
> Anybody want to buy a paper?

JENNIE:
> Hey, Joeie's here with the Nugget . . . pass the hat round for Joeie! Isn't he a dear?

The PROSPECTOR starts round with the hat for
JOEIE as JENNIE puts her arm round JOEIE.

His da froze and his mum takes in washin'. He's
sweet Jennie's dear, aren't you, Joeie? You're sweet
Jennie's sweetheart, aren't you?

The PROSPECTOR approaches WALSH after
collecting from others.

PROSPECTOR: *holds out the hat*
For Joeie.

WALSH looks at him. There is something of incom-
prehension in his gaze.

I'm askin' for somethin' for the little boy.

WALSH:
I can give you nothing.

PROSPECTOR:
You and your kind have taken enough off us — you
kin spare somethin' for the little boy.

WALSH:
I can give you nothing!

PROSPECTOR:
It ain't enough you're a son-of-a-bitch — you gotta
be a cheap son-of-a-bitch!

WALSH hits him in the face knocking him down. As
he goes to get up, WALSH plants a foot in his back
and sends him sprawling.

CLARENCE: *screams from the shadows*
NOOOOOOOOO!

There is a freeze with WALSH with his hand upraised to hit the PROSPECTOR, IAN with the bottle raised as a club, JENNIE drawing JOEIE to her. All of the characters in the saloon in positions of action with the exception of HARRY who is a spectator. There is a pause, then HARRY steps forward moving among the frozen characters.

HARRY: *addresses the audience*
The Klondike! Eighteen ninety-eight! And the end for Major James A. Walsh, formerly of the North West Mounted Police, an original member of the First Contingent of that Force, formed in 1873 by Sir John A. MacDonald to police the Canadian West! *He smashes fist on table. The freeze ends.*

HARRY continues as actors leave. Major Walsh never met General Custer, which was kinda a pity 'cause the day Custer met Sittin' Bull was the beginnin' of the end for Major Walsh . . . Old Glory Hound Custer — now he had a fail-proof plan for killin' off Injuns. First off, you found yourself some friendlies. You was forced to kill friendlies cause it was too difficult findin' hostiles, but friendlies camped near the forts, to show their good-will kinda like, and it weren't too hard to come across a bunch of 'em set up in some cozy little hollow, flyin' the 'merican flag for good measure. *dry chuckle* Well now once you picked yourself some Injuns, you gotta pick yourself a time. Custer thought winter was the best, for the Injun had always figured fightin' in the winter wasn't sportin' like, and avoided it if he could . . . Custer was an early riser; and if you team up a winter date with a 4 a.m. charge when the Injuns was all asleep, you pretty well had it made . . . Course tactics comes into it, Custer did all right there too. 'Member that cozy little hollow I mentioned? Sorta a tube-like hollow was best, cause what you did was send a bunch of men in one end of the tube, and course all hell broke loose there, what with kids screamin', women runnin', and men lookin' for somethin' to hit back with, and the whole works naked as the day they was born, it bein' the middle of the night as far as they was concerned. Anyway, as their attention was somewhat di-verted by this here attack at one end of the tube, Custer, with a bunch of the boys, would sneak round t'other end, and ride through, hell-bent for whoop-up, killin' off the strays, and generally gettin' a lot of 'em in the back while they was lookin' t'other way . . . It were a pretty efficient way to fight a war . . . The flag did its bit too, for the Injuns was prone to rally under it thinkin' maybe the fact they was friendly had been missed; occas-sionally one of 'em even had time to run up a white flag. *reminiscent* There was almost a kinda festive at-mos-phere to a Custer attack what with his marchin' band playing "Garryowen". Custer liked to charge to music, and "Garryowen" was his favourite, although he was fond of "The Girl I Left Behind" too . . . Still, generally, it was "Garryowen".

He whistles a few bars of "Garryowen". It begins brightly, but becomes slower and slower, then stops. Silence for a second. Not as light as the first part of the monologue.

The Little Big Horn . . . June 25th . . . 1876 . . .
First off, wrong time — June ain't December, and that's a fact. Just shows how success kin go to your head. And the Injuns at the Little Big Horn weren't friendly. They was hostile. They was hostile as hell. Sittin' Bull and the Sioux had listened to the 'merican government say, "The utmost good faith shall always be observed towards the Indians, and their land and property shall never be taken from them without their consent." They had taken the government at its word — bein' savages they weren't too familiar with governments and all, so it was an understandable mistake.

So we got wrong month, and wrong bunch of Injuns. These Sioux weren't sittin' under no flag waitin' to be popped off like passenger pigeons . . . On June 25th, Custer was up at 4 a.m. all right, trouble was he never found no Injuns till noon time. His fail-proof plan for killin' off Injuns was goin' to hell in a hand basket. On top of everythin' else, the marchin' band had a prior engagement with General Terry.

So here's Custer . . . at noontime . . . in late June . . . with no marchin' band comin' upon a camp of hostiles. Well now, it weren't hardly a camp either, it was a gathering-together, under Sittin' Bull, of the last of those Injuns who weren't willin' to swap their huntin' grounds and freedom for a small corner of a reservation, 'bout 4,000 warriors plus women and children. And what they was camped in wasn't by no stretch of the imagination a tube-like hollow; it was a gentle rollin' sweep of Montana prairie.

Custer, seein' it was gettin' later in the day by the minute, and probably wantin' to avoid that early afternoon slump most early risers suffer from, decided to attack without sendin' out a scout to see just how far this here camp of Injuns extended. He had 'bout 500 men, and he figured that would be enough with some left over . . . "Take no prisoners" was the order . . . Major Reno, who, incidentally, had never fought Injuns before, only other 'mericans in the Civil War, this here Reno was given the honour of ridin' with 'bout half the men into one end of the non-tube. Which he did. And got the bejesus beat out of him. He made a hasty retreat to a bluff where he sat with his men for 2 days cursin' Custer for runnin' off and leavin' them to the mercy of the Injuns and the sun. Forgot to mention that Custer did have this unfortunate habit of cuttin' his losses and ridin' off.

This time Custer hadn't riden off; he wasn't goin' nowhere; he'd taken his half of the 7th, ridden a couple of miles, and cut down to what he figured was the outskirts of the camp. Two miles. His figurin' was 'bout 8 miles out. He found Injuns aplenty, and none of them was facin' the other way . . .

On June 28th, General Terry came on a yellow-brown slope dotted with dead horses and pale white bodies — the dead — stripped of arms, ammunition, equipment — and clothin' . . . At the summit of the slope stood a horse. The sole survivor of Custer's Last Stand was a clay-coloured horse, Comanche, still on his feet with 10 bullet holes in him. The bullet holes eventually healed, and on April 10th, 1878, the horse was commissioned "second commandin' officer" of the 7th Cavalry, and on all occasions of ceremony saddled, bridled, draped in mournin', and led by a mounted trooper, Comanche paraded with the regiment . . . I hear tell, that when Terry looked on Custer's dead body, he wept, and said. "The flower of the American Army is gone."

Well now, the rest of the 'merican Army was out to avenge the "Custer massacre." Sittin' Bull and the Sioux were hard to lay hands on, but there was always the friendlies.

Act One

The action continues without a break.

HARRY: *begins to move treaty goods*
Across the line, in the country of the Great White
Mother, Major James A. Walsh of the North West
Mounted was enforcin' law and order as decreed by
Her Majesty's Government.

CLARENCE: *offstage*
Hey Harry!

HARRY:
I had . . . what you might call vacated the U-nited
States, and had myself a job as wagon master . . .

CLARENCE: *offstage*
Harry! What're you doin'? Come on!

HARRY:

I'm comin'! I was runnin' treaty goods for Canadian Injuns into Fort Walsh.

CLARENCE: *offstage*

Jesus Christ, Harry! Would you give me a hand!

HARRY: *without moving to go*

I said, I'm comin'!

CLARENCE:

Never mind, you lazy bastard! *grunts and groans of effort* I'll do it myself!

HARRY:

Be right with you.

CLARENCE enters bent double under a packing case. HARRY sits and watches him.

Hey, you better watch out for . . .

CLARENCE trips over ploughshare, falls flat with case spilling shovels out.

. . . the ploughshare.

CLARENCE sits up, looking 'round at shovels, cases, etc.

CLARENCE: *speaks plaintively*

What the hell are they goin' to do with these?

HARRY: *matter-of-fact*

Nothin'.

CLARENCE:

What do you mean, nothin'?

HARRY: *explaining a fact of life*
They're gonna do nothin' with these. We're gonna haul 'em all over here, your Major's gonna pass 'em all out, and they're gonna haul 'em all away — and they ain't gonna do nothin' with 'em. The seeds' gonna rot, the 'shares gonna rust, and them god damn shovels is just gonna lie where they flung 'em.

CLARENCE:
If they aren't gonna use 'em, why're we luggin' them around?

HARRY:
I'll tell you somethin'. Your Major's gonna be madder than a wet hen when he sees this lot. Second lot I brung in this month. First lot, the Major, he threw a real fit, said he was gonna write the Prime Minister, tell 'im to stuff his farm u-tensils.

CLARENCE:
Hey, did you hear the talk over at the fort?

HARRY bites off chaw of tobacco, looks at CLARENCE disdainfully.

HARRY:
That talk's everywhere, Clarence.

CLARENCE:
Do you believe it?

HARRY:
Don't see why it couldn't be true.

CLARENCE:
Aren't you scared?

HARRY:
Now why'd I be scared, Clarence?

CLARENCE:
We're gonna have ourselves an Injun War, just like
the States, that's why!

HARRY gives him a dry look.

The Sioux are headed north . . . An Injun War! . . .
I could get to kill the man who killed Custer!

HARRY:
And who might that be?

CLARENCE:
Why, Sittin' Bull, of course.

HARRY:
How'd you know it was him personally killed Custer?

CLARENCE: *defensive*
Well . . . everybody says so! It was Sittin' Bull himself killed Custer at the Little Big Horn — with
his huntin' knife! *thinks about it and backs down a
bit* I guess the only ones know for sure are the men
who died with Custer, eh?

HARRY: *politely*
Ain't you forgettin' somethin'?

CLARENCE:
What?

HARRY:
I seem to recollect there was some other people
present at that event.

CLARENCE:
Who?

HARRY:
> Jesus Christ, Clarence! The Indians, that's who! You think a white man's the only person kin know anythin' for sure! Whyn't you try askin' an Injun who killed Custer! You bleedin' redcoats don't know nothin'!

CLARENCE: *insulted*
> You wanna fight!

> *HARRY looks at CLARENCE, directs spittle of 'baccy juice at CLARENCE's feet. CLARENCE hauls back his fist.*

LOUIS: *from shadows, to CLARENCE*
> 'Ey!

WALSH: *enters, his attention fixed on crates*
> What the hell's this?

HARRY: *clears his throat*
> Well, sir, I 'spect you'd say . . . it was more . . .

WALSH:
> And this . . . and this . . . and this! *slapping each item with his riding crop*

LOUIS: *attempting to be helpful*
> 'Dat's ploughshare, we got 'em last time.

WALSH:
> I know we got them last time — why're we getting them this time!

> *LOUIS shrugs.*

> *WALSH's glance falls on CLARENCE. He really notices him for the first time. CLARENCE feels obliged to say something.*

CLARENCE:
I . . . I don't know, sir.

WALSH: *irritation seems to go, and his manner changes*
Ah, new recruit, aren't you?

CLARENCE:
Yes sir.

WALSH:
Name?

CLARENCE:
Constable Clarence Underhill, sir!

WALSH:
Welcome to the fort, Constable. Keep your eyes, ears, and mind open . . .

CLARENCE:
Yes s. . .

WALSH:
And your mouth shut. *turns to HARRY, friendly*
All right, Harry. *leans on crate beside HARRY*
What is all this? *indicating equipment with crop*

HARRY:
Well, sir . . .

WALSH: *exceedingly friendly*
Some immigrant family ordered it, I suppose . . .

HARRY:
Ah . . . I can't rightly say that, sir.

WALSH:
Aha . . . then you're taking it up to Calgary, are you, for some poor witless farmer there.

HARRY:
No sir . . . not that either.

WALSH:
Mmnn . . . planning on homesteading yourself, are you?

HARRY: *smiles, the idea amuses him*
Not very likely, sir.

WALSH stares at HARRY for a second. He lowers his voice and the speech builds.

WALSH:
Are you telling me, man, that once again, the government has seen fit to burden me and the natives of these parts with another load of seed and equipment to rot and rust, when they know god damn well, because I've told them time and again, that these Indians are not, and never will be, farmers!

Pause as WALSH stares at HARRY.

HARRY: *weakly*
That's it, sir.

WALSH:
Right! . . . *anger seems to subside* Well . . . can't be helped, can it. *He walks 'round crate tapping it with his riding crop, then barks:* Bill of lading! *extends his hand*

CLARENCE: *starts*
Ah! Yes sir!

He feels pocket as WALSH watches expressionless. He finds bill, presents it to WALSH, but not quite in his hand, and it begins to float to the ground. CLARENCE retrieves it, places it in WALSH's hand.

WALSH: *drily*
Thank you, Constable.

CLARENCE:
Yes sir!

WALSH looks at CLARENCE, then moves away with HARRY.

WALSH:
What all have you got here, Harry? *He and HARRY begin to check the number of crates.*

LOUIS looks over to CLARENCE.

LOUIS:
'Ey . . . 'ey dere . . . *beckons with his finger*

CLARENCE moves over to him although he's still more or less at attention and focused on WALSH in case he should suddenly want something.

Dis . . . a . . . first time you meet da . . . *nods towards WALSH* . . . commandin' officer up close, eh?

CLARENCE nods, looks at LOUIS warily. LOUIS looks somewhat disreputable in his "scout" outfit.

What you think of 'im?

CLARENCE:
He seems a little . . . *casts a nervous glance to WALSH*

WALSH: *to HARRY*
Read it yourself! *thrusts bill at HARRY* What does that look like to you?

CLARENCE smiles weakly at LOUIS who smiles back.

HARRY:
It, ah, looks like we're missin' one crate, Major.

WALSH:
I trust you'll find it.

HARRY:
I'll do that, yes I will, Major. First thing I hit Fort MacLeod.

WALSH:
Right. *takes bill and begins to check it against goods listed on outside of crates* . . . so . . . contents . . . *HARRY assists.*

LOUIS: *indicating himself*
Louis Leveille. *shakes hands with CLARENCE* Fort Walsh scout . . . Mother red, father white . . . but not so white as da Major dere . . . Louis' father French. *He laughs. CLARENCE realizes it's a joke and smiles back.*

WALSH:
Mark it off! Mark it off!

HARRY does so, CLARENCE glances at them nervously.

LOUIS:
Ah — don't worry — mean nothin' — just 'is way. He care a lot and so he yell a lot, eh?

CLARENCE:
Yeah. I guess you gotta know a lot to be an officer.

LOUIS:
Louis tell yuh somethin' . . . Take all da books, da news dat da white man prints, take all dat bible book, take all dose things you learn from — lay dem on da prairie — and da sun . . . da rain . . . da snow . . .

pouf! You wanna learn, you study inside here *taps head* ... and here *taps chest* ... and how it is wit' you and me *indicates* ... and how it is wit' you and all. *indicates surroundings* Travel 'round da Medicine Wheel. Den you know somethin'.

WALSH: *approaching CLARENCE and LOUIS*
Well, Louis, there's another lot, courtesy of those fools in Ottawa.

LOUIS:
Dose fools that're sittin' dere ain't such fools as da people dat sent dem dere, eh Major? *chuckles from WALSH*

HARRY begins to clear treaty goods.

MRS. ANDERSON: *offstage*
Major Walsh! Oh Major!

WALSH sighs. MRS. ANDERSON enters almost hysterical.

Major Walsh!

WALSH: *smiles at her*
Yes, Mrs. Anderson.

MRS. ANDERSON: *almost in tears*
Major Walsh, the most terrible thing has happened.

CROW EAGLE enters with great dignity. He is a bit ahead of Sergeant McCUTCHEON. He is in custody although no hand is on him.

WALSH:
Now it's all right, Mrs. Anderson. Just tell us what this is all about.

MRS. ANDERSON:
Ah Major, this savage . . . this heathen . . . this . . .
Indian has stolen my washtub!

*A pained expression passes over WALSH's face, he
shakes his head, makes an almost inaudible tut-tut
sound.*

Yes. It was right outside the door, and these heathens
snuck up and stole it. I'm counting on you, Major,
to return that tub! I mean, what am I to rinse in,
otherwise?

WALSH:
Well, Crow Eagle, did you take this white lady's tub?

CROW EAGLE:
That is so.

MRS. ANDERSON:
What did I tell you? *circles CROW EAGLE in rage*
Mark my words, they'll be killing us in our sleep
next!

WALSH: *placating*
Mrs. Anderson . . . *to CROW EAGLE* Why'd you
take the tub?

CROW EAGLE:
We needed a drum.

WALSH:
The Great White Mother'd be very angry if she
discovered you'd taken this white lady's washtub.

CROW EAGLE:
I am sure if the Great White Mother knew how much
we needed that drum, she would be glad to let us
keep it.

MRS. ANDERSON:
As if the Queen cared about them!

CROW EAGLE:
We have cut the bottom out of that tub, and covered it with buffalo skin. It makes a very good drum.

LOUIS:
Da white lady has 'nother tub — why does she not use dat?

MRS. ANDERSON: *goes to seize CROW EAGLE's arm*
What's mine's my own! You'll not take . . .
WALSH takes her arm drawing her aside.

WALSH:
Mrs. Anderson!

MRS. ANDERSON:
Whose side are you on, Jim?

WALSH:
I was unaware we were choosing sides. My job is to keep the peace and see that justice is done.

MRS. ANDERSON:
Then get me my tub!

WALSH: *a trifle tired*
Louis, explain it to him.

LOUIS: *begins to explain in Cree*
Na-mo-ya ta-ki otin-a-man ki-kwhy a-ka a-tipay-hitaman . . . *(It is not lawful to take what is not your own) . . .*

CROW EAGLE: *dismissing LOUIS and speaking to WALSH*
White Forehead Chief!! Why we should not keep it?

WALSH: *after a pause*
You must not take articles from the whites again.
They need even what they appear not to need . . .
And you must bring skins in payment for the . . .
drum . . . Make sure he understands, Louis.

*LOUIS draws CROW EAGLE to one side in muffled
conversation, in background to WALSH's next speech.*

LOUIS:
Wapi-ka-tik-oki-maw it-o-wew-may-scootch ata-yuk
ta-pa-so-wa-chik to tippo-what misti-kwa-shihk-asa
kotin-nut. *(The White Forehead Chief says you must
bring skins in payment for the drum you have taken).*

CROW EAGLE:
Ni-ka-to-tayn namaya-ni-nistotayn ma-ka ni-ka-to-
tayn keespin Wapi-ka-tik ekosi it-o-wew-ni-ka-to-
tayn. *(I will do it. I do not understand it, but I will
do it. If the White Forehead Chief says it . . . I will
do it).*

LOUIS:
Pi-ko ta-na-hi-ta-wat Okimaskoew Kwa-yask ta-pa-
mi-hayew ki-ta-yis-si-ni-ma apo tchi ke-yom ta-wan-
kiski-sew kiya. *(You must obey the Great White
Mother's law. She will look after your people if you
do — otherwise she will forget you).*

CROW EAGLE:
Wapi-ka-tik chee pa-taw aso-ta-ma-to-aina paski-
si-gana, mosiniya nin-ta wahitaynan paskowaw
mastosak aya-wak sa-ka-staynok. *(Has she sent the
White Forehead Chief the goods that I asked for my
people? We need ammunition, we have seen buffalo
to the south).*

*WALSH takes MRS. ANDERSON's arm and steers
her away slightly.*

31

WALSH:

Now look, Emma . . .

MRS. ANDERSON:

What about my tub?

WALSH:

Emma — the Indians, they see two tubs in your yard.
You have to remember they've a different background
from us . . .

MRS. ANDERSON:

Background? They don't have any background.

WALSH:

Well, as I was saying . . .

MRS. ANDERSON:

Are you telling me I'm not getting my tub back?

WALSH:

That's right, Emma.

MRS. ANDERSON:

What will you do when they murder us in our beds?
You're nothing but a . . .

WALSH:

Would you have me throw him in chains! To hell
with your damned old tub! We're not going to start
an Indian war over it!

MRS. ANDERSON:

No! You'll sit by and let the Sioux do that!

*She whirls and exits. WALSH stands stiff and tense
as she exits, then we see him relax and turn to
McCUTCHEON. He smiles, sighs and shakes his
head.*

WALSH:
The Sioux . . . Well, McCutcheon . . . Hell hath no fury like a woman deprived of her wash tub. *walks around equipment looking at it casually* You'd think it was her very existence.

McCUTCHEON:
Aye sir. You're right there. I tell ye I'd rather face a hostile in a fit of pique than Mrs. Anderson with her dander up . . .

LOUIS:
Crow Eagle asks for ammunition to hunt da buffalo. His scouts have seen a small herd to da south.

WALSH:
Every year there're fewer buffalo, and soon there will be no more. His people must think of next year and the year after.

LOUIS: *almost gently*
Ever since he was born he has eaten wild meat. His father and his grandfather ate wild meat. He cannot give up quickly the customs of his fathers.

WALSH: *directly to CROW EAGLE, a bit more formal*
When the white man comes, the buffalo goes . . . And with the buffalo goes the life you have known. You cannot stop this happening any more than you can stop the sun or the moon. You must find a new life . . . That is why the Great White Mother sends you these . . . *indicates equipment* . . . So you can start a New Life.

CROW EAGLE:
I do not wish to be servant to a cow.

HARRY: *laughs*
He's got somethin' there . . .

WALSH:
Yes, well . . . McCutcheon, take him over to the post and see he gets ammunition for the hunt.

McCUTCHEON:
Aye sir.

They go to leave.

WALSH:
Crow Eagle, you must think of the time when there are no more buffalo.

CROW EAGLE:
When there are no more buffalo — there are no more Indians.

He and McCUTCHEON exit. WALSH watches them leave.

WALSH: *to himself*
I ask you, can you see that man bent double over a hoe?

HARRY:
Don't appear likely they'll ever be farmers, that's a fact.

WALSH:
Farmers? Not farmers! If they're to grow anything in this dust bowl, the government'll have to turn them into magicians!

CLARENCE: *stands at attention*
Excuse me, sir . . . permission to speak, sir.

WALSH appears almost lost in thought as he gazes after CROW EAGLE.

WALSH:
Yes . . . what is it?

CLARENCE:
There's been some talk, sir, among the men at the post . . . about the hostiles from the States.

WALSH: *still not particularly attentive*
Go on . . .

CLARENCE: *encouraged*
About them comin' up into Canada — Sittin' Bull and the whole Sioux Nation comin' up into Canada to get away from the U.S. Army . . .

Sometime during the speech we see that WALSH is alert and listening.

WALSH:
Yes?

CLARENCE:
Well . . . I was just wonderin', sir, if that was true . . . I mean, the whole Sioux Nation, sir? And we only got 'bout 60 men here . . .

WALSH:
Yes.

CLARENCE:
. . . and you know . . . I'm not askin' for myself, sir, it's just that I'd like to write a last letter home to me mum if we . . . if we were on the verge of war, sir, or anything like that . . . sir.

WALSH: *speaks quietly*
What have the Sioux done?

35

CLARENCE: *blurts out*
They killed Custer!

WALSH:
And Custer killed them.

CLARENCE:
Yes sir.

WALSH:
What have the Sioux done to us?

CLARENCE looks nervously to HARRY, then back to WALSH.

CLARENCE:
Nothin', sir?

WALSH:
In which case, I don't believe we're on the verge of war with them. *lightly* What do you say, Louis?

LOUIS: *smiles*
I think out redcoats too damn busy chasin' 'merican whiskey traders. Dey much worse trouble dan any Sioux I run across.

WALSH: *smiles*
My sentiments exactly. *He and LOUIS start off.*

The sound of the Sioux's arrival creeps in very softly — muted voices, horses, faint drums and singing. It can bearly be heard.

CLARENCE:
Sir!

WALSH: *turning back to him*
Yes, Constable.

CLARENCE: *quickly*
> Request permission to accompany the Major when he rides out to meet Sittin' Bull and the Sioux, sir!

WALSH:
> What about that letter to your mother?

CLARENCE:
> I'll write it tonight, sir.

WALSH: *has a hard time keeping a smile off his face*
> Permission granted.

> *WALSH exits as CLARENCE tense and HARRY casual watch him. Then CLARENCE looks at HARRY — grins, relaxes, leaps into the air, throws hat off. There's a certain similarity to an Indian youth out for his first coup.*

CLARENCE:
> Yip yip yip yip yipeeeeeeeeeeeeeeeee! Whahooo!

> *HARRY and CLARENCE exit. Lights dim as LOUIS crouches listening to sound which builds. LOUIS moves about as if watching the Sioux's arrival. The sound is well established before he speaks.*

LOUIS:
> Tabernacle!   *casts a glance over his shoulder*   Major! Dis way!

> *WALSH and McCUTCHEON enter. They are standing on a slight rise.*

> See . . . da village is dere.   *indicates a direction*
> Dat dust, dat is more joinin' dose already camped.

> *WALSH hands his binoculars to McCUTCHEON. WALSH gazes at the village using only the naked eye as the scout does.*

WALSH:
>Must be . . . what . . . 2 miles away. What would you say, Louis?

LOUIS: *smiles*
>Louis say you damn good pupil.

WALSH: *smiles*
>Louis damn good teacher.

McCUTCHEON: *looking through binoculars — lowers them*
>Must be 2,000 people there.

LOUIS:
>Maybeso 5,000.

CLARENCE: *enters*
>The horses're picketed, sir.

>*WALSH turns to CLARENCE. He speaks quickly with an intensity that indicates he is taut as a bow string and ready for anything.*

WALSH:
>You wanted to see the Sioux, Constable — all right, here they come. I want you to remember something. You do not draw your gun unless you see me draw mine. You will follow orders exactly, precisely, and immediately. If you do one thing that precipitates trouble between us and the Sioux, you need not worry about a redskin taking your scalp. I myself will place a bullet between your eyes faster than you can say write-a-letter-home. *a threat he means* Do you understand?

>*For the first time CLARENCE is aware of the potential explosiveness of the situation.*

CLARENCE:
>I do, sir.

The sound is building.

WALSH:

Louis, beside me . . . McCutcheon and Underhill behind . . .

They take up their positions. WALSH gives a quick look to CLARENCE. I rely on you to uphold the honour of the Force.

Sound is at crescendo, all around the audience, for several seconds. It stops. A pause.

GALL enters, followed by SITTING BULL who looks austere, has one feather in his hair. They stop a short distance from WALSH. WALSH raises his hand, palm outward. GALL returns gesture. Silence for a second.

Louis, tell them . . .

GALL:

We speak as men — to each other. *meaning he does not need an interpreter* I am Gall of the Hunkpapa Lakota.

WALSH:

You've crossed the line into the country of the Great White Mother.

GALL stares at WALSH impassively.

SITTING BULL follows conversation. His movements, if any, are slow and deliberate. He was a man of great presence and personal magnetism. It was not necessary for him to speak or to draw attention to himself in any way for one to be aware of his strength of character. It was his custom to carefully size up a situation before committing himself to an action.

I am a soldier of the Great White Mother. You may know me and others like me, by my red coat. *indicates his tunic*

GALL: *offers WALSH a George III medal*
My grandfather was a soldier for the grandfather of Queen Victoria. At that time your people told him that the Sioux Nation belonged to that grandfather of the Queen. My people fought against the Longknives for your people then. We were told that you would always look after your Red Children. Now The Longknives have stolen our land. We have no place to go. We come home to you asking for that protection you promised.

WALSH takes medal from GALL, examines it, looks at GALL. WALSH is not actually prepared for this specific argument for Canada's obligation to the Sioux.

McCUTCHEON: *quietly*
What is it, sir?

WALSH: *passes medal to McCUTCHEON*
It's a George III medal — the Sioux fought for the British in 1776 against the Americans.

He looks at GALL and speaks carefully — his orders from Ottawa have not covered this exigency.

We are your friends, that is true . . .

GALL:
The Lakota has need of friends. I want you to know this trouble was not begun by us. The Longknives have come out of the night, and for campfires they have lit our lodges. Our women weep, and the nostrils of our babies must be pinched lest they cry out and give us away. At the Greasy Grass, the Long Hair attacked our camp, and we rose up like the

buffalo bull when the cows are attacked and we rubbed him out. Now we are hunted as we hunt animals . . . and we have crossed the line.

LOUIS: *nudges WALSH*
'Ey — on the ridge — is dat not da horses of Pere de Corbay?

WALSH: *looks, frowns, indicates hills*
Whose horses graze there?

GALL: *looks*
White Dog's, our Assiniboin Brother.

WALSH:
I wish to speak to him.

Sound of rattles, drums.

GALL leaves. CLARENCE shifts nervously. McCUTCHEON gives him a look.

McCUTCHEON: *in a low voice*
Easy, laddie.

CLARENCE: *takes a slow look over his shoulder*
We're bloody well surrounded, Sergeant.

McCUTCHEON:
Never ye mind, laddie. Just keep your eye on the Major.

WALSH takes a slow walk. He whistles. He stops, looking at SITTING BULL.

WALSH:
Gall! *GALL turns towards him.*   I ask the name of the man who stands with us.

GALL:
>A wise man . . .

WHITE DOG enters. He carries a rifle in one hand.

WALSH: *quickly*
>McCutcheon.

WHITE DOG: *belligerent*
>White Dog?!

WALSH:
>The horses on the ridge, are they yours?

WHITE DOG: *antagonistic*
>You say!

WALSH: *snaps out*
>McCutcheon!

McCUTCHEON moves briskly, seizes WHITE DOG's arms. WHITE DOG resists, but McCUTCHEON holds him immobile. WALSH's hand rests easily, almost casually on his holstered gun. As McCUTCHEON seizes WHITE DOG, WHITE DOG cries out. There is a swell of sound from the surrounding Sioux we cannot see. WALSH raises his voice and announces as the sound continues BG.

>Those are the horses of Pere de Corbay! His brand can be seen from here! White Dog is under arrest for stealing!

WHITE DOG:
>I find loose! It is custom horses taken! No law!

WALSH: *after a pause*
>Release him! *McCUTCHEON does so.* Next time you find horses not belonging to you, they must be left alone!

WHITE DOG: *as he turns to leave he calls back threateningly*
Meet again, Wichitas!

WALSH:
White Dog! *walks up to WHITE DOG oblivious of his rifle* Repeat your words.

WHITE DOG: *a coward*
Meet again sometime!

WALSH: *speaks quietly, but not without menace*
Take back those words.

WHITE DOG hesitates a minute, then looks to SITTING BULL — back to WALSH.

WHITE DOG:
White Dog not threaten.

WALSH: *inclines his head slightly*
Then go, I have no grudge against White Dog.

WHITE DOG hurries off. The BG noise swells. WALSH walks to SITTING BULL who raises his hand. The noise stops.

SITTING BULL:
These people are my people — I am Sitting Bull.

WALSH:
Major James Walsh of the North West Mounted Police. *He extends his hand, after a second's hesitation, SITTING BULL takes it.*

SITTING BULL:
My people need ammunition.

WALSH: *begins his "government" statement*
The Queen will not tolerate raiding from her soil, nor does she . . .

SITTING BULL:
Hard times have come to us. My warriors use the lasso to bring down meat.

WALSH: *stares at him for a split second, decides he trusts him*
Ammunition will be issued sufficient for hunting purposes. McCutcheon, take the Constable and see to it.

McCUTCHEON:
Aye sir.

McCUTCHEON and CLARENCE exit. The lights begin to dim.

SITTING BULL:
We shall meet again.

WALSH: *smiles*
I look forward to it.

GALL, WALSH, and SITTING BULL exit.

PRETTY PLUME enters, unrolls buffalo skin for floor of tent as LOUIS, singing softly, removes his pack and sits a distance from the "tent."

En roulant ma boule roulant, enroulant ma boule.
En roulant ma boule roulant, enroulant ma boule.
Derrier' chez nous, y'a-t'un e-tang, enroulant ma boule,
Trois beaux canards s'en vont baignant, roulant ma boule, roulant.

Lights brighten as McCUTCHEON and CLARENCE enter, carrying bowls of food. McCUTCHEON passes one to LOUIS.

McCUTCHEON:
Here y'are, Louis.

McCUTCHEON and CLARENCE sit, all three begin to eat. LOUIS eats with relish, McCUTCHEON simply eats, and CLARENCE sloshes his bowl around peering into it with apprehension. He is reassured by LOUIS' appreciation of the contents, CLARENCE dips his fingers in, comes up with something unpleasant. He quickly drops it back and grimaces. He looks at McCUTCHEON who tilts his bowl a bit and drains it. CLARENCE swallows, and looks down at his bowl. LOUIS glances over at him.

LOUIS:
Dat some good, eh?   *teasing CLARENCE*

CLARENCE smiles weakly and nods half-heartedly. LOUIS gets up. 'Nother one?   *holds out his hand to take bowl*

McCUTCHEON: *puts his empty bowl down*
Not for me, Louis.

CLARENCE: *as LOUIS looks at him*
I . . . still got some, thanks anyway.

LOUIS exits to get some more.

McCUTCHEON: *calls after him*
My compliments to the chef, Louis!

CLARENCE stares at McCUTCHEON, then down at his own bowl. McCUTCHEON suppresses a smile.

Laddie, ye better be eatin' that up, if ye want to keep your forelock.

CLARENCE:
What do you mean?

McCUTCHEON: *whispers*
> It's a great insult to not eat what's put before ye when y're visitin' the Sioux . . . Men have been known to lose their scalps over such an insult.

CLARENCE: *sickly*
> That so?

> *He dips his fingers in, comes in contact with something unpleasant, drops it back, sits for a second, then makes up his mind.*

> Well, I don't give a damn! I'd sooner be scalped than eat any more of this stuff! Here, you take it.

McCUTCHEON: *laughs, pushes the bowl away*
> I've done my duty, laddie, now it's up to you.

LOUIS: *returns, dejected*
> Merde, McCutch. Dey eat it all up. Dere's none left.

CLARENCE: *looks up, brightens*
> Say, Louis, I think . . . *feels his own forehead* . . . I think I overdid it a bit today, don't really feel too much like eatin' tonight . . . If you want mine, well, no sense seein' it wasted. *offers his bowl hopefully*

LOUIS: *smiles, recognizing CLARENCE's ploy*
> Dat so? Weeeelllll . . . *takes bowl, squats down, eats*

CLARENCE smiles at McCUTCHEON.

McCUTCHEON:
> Now I wonder how the Major's makin' out.

LOUIS: *looks up*
Da Major and Sittin' Bull's over in da big tipi dere.
Dey send Louis away, but he keep an eye out all da
same. *back to his food*

*McCUTCHEON get out his pipe, stretches his legs,
remains sitting.*

McCUTCHEON:
The Sioux have behaved themselves, there's no
denyin' that. Six months it's been, and they're as
good as gold.

LOUIS puts down his bowl, looks at McCUTCHEON.

LOUIS:
Dese Sioux, dey not stupid, you know. Make trouble
and dey know what happens. 'Mericans send Longknives up here. Dey kill every Indian dey see — little
ones, big ones, mama with bebe — dey don't give
good god damn, friendly or hostile . . . You got red
skin . . . *points finger* . . . bang-bang! . . . Louis'
skin got reddish tinge. *an awkward silence*

*The lights dim a bit. McCUTCHEON and CLARENCE
look down, LOUIS shrugs, gets out his pipe.*

McCUTCHEON: *passes LOUIS his pouch of tobacco*
Try mine.

LOUIS: *takes it, fingers it*
You buy new one, eh?

McCUTCHEON:
I got it at the post before we left. Feel that leather,
soft, isn't it?

LOUIS:

> Dat's nice . . . *gazes off into space* . . . but not so nice as 'nother pouch I saw once . . . many year ago, before the redcoats come, I saw white man at Fort Whoop-Up, a Longknife . . . He show everybody mighty nice tobacco pouch he have . . . made from breast of Indian woman he killed at Sand Creek.

> *He looks in direction of SITTING BULL's tipi. McCUTCHEON and CLARENCE follow suit. As lights dim on them they begin to come up on SITTING BULL's tipi. There is a soft BG sound of Indian rattles and bells which continues BG till SITTING BULL scene is established.*

> *WALSH and SITTING BULL are eating. WALSH looks up from his bowl after a moment.*

WALSH:

> . . . Louis tells me you've been visitin' the Blackfoot and the Cree.

SITTING BULL:

> They tell me that Major Walsh is the White Forehead Chief, and the White Forehead Chief is the Indian's friend. If trouble strikes your camp, they say send for the White Forehead Chief.

WALSH:

> The Blackfoot . . .

SITTING BULL:

> Do you ride out to speak only of the Blackfoot and the Cree — have you no news for the Sioux?

WALSH:

> Yes, I have news — and it's not good news . . . My chief says the Queen is not responsible for you. *holds up George III medal* This happened a long time ago. The Great White Mother has made peace with the Americans.

SITTING BULL: *hint of sarcasm*

Whose "Red Children" are we, then?

WALSH:

It was decided the Sioux belonged to the President in Washington.

SITTING BULL:

It was decided . . . You are few, and we are many. Will you try to drive us back across the line?

WALSH:

You're welcome to stay here so long as your young men don't cross the line to raid, and so long as the Sioux are self-sufficient . . . The Queen won't feed or clothe you as she does her own Indians.

SITTING BULL: *leaning towards WALSH*

My people have never accepted the annuities — we have never touched the pen — we have never sold our land! It has been stolen from us. You need not feed or clothe us. The Hunkpapa Lakota feed and clothe themselves!

WALSH: *gently*

Soon you won't be able to do that. The buffalo will be gone. You must return to your home before that happens.

SITTING BULL:

The Black Hills is our home! And the white man has stolen them! I cannot sign away the Black Hills. They are not mine alone. Before me, they were my father's. After me, they shall be my children's. Do you sign away the birthright of your children?

WALSH:

I tell you this because I am a soldier, and I must follow orders, but I am friend also. White Forehead *indicating himself* does not say this; Major Walsh

says this. *official*   The President in Washington
has requested the Sioux to return, and promises fair
treatment to all.

*SITTING BULL stares at WALSH for a moment,
then begins conversationally, casually.*

SITTING BULL:
Let me tell you what I have heard today . . . Today
I have news of my good friend Crazy Horse of the
Oglala. He was a dreamer wishing only to serve his
people, and they loved him well . . . Brave in battle.
Wise in council. He loved the little children and
could not bear to see them suffer. The Oglala and
the Hunkpapa fought together at the Greasy Grass
where Custer died. I brought my people across the
line, but Crazy Horse and the Oglala remained behind.
Since that time, they've known no peace. General
Terry pursued them like a wolf who tears at the soft
underbelly of a fleeing doe. . . There are two reservation chiefs across the line named Red Cloud and
Spotted Tail. Some say they are paper chiefs created
by the white man to betray their Red Brothers . . .
Red Cloud and Spotted Tail met Crazy Horse in
council, and begged him to bring his people in, to
touch the pen, to lead a reservation life. They told
him, "You will be a great chief!" . . . The Sioux are
proud, we love position . . . My good friend Crazy
Horse is dead. He brought his people in, and when
he stepped into the meeting place, he saw the win-
dows all were barred, and 'round about stood soldiers
pointing long knives at him; and when he turned to
run, his arms were pinioned by his Red Brothers, and
a white soldier pushed his bayonet into Crazy Horse's
stomach! It took one night for him to die. He sang
his death song and his mother and father stood outside and sang back for the white soldiers would not
let them enter where he lay dying. And where he
stood when he was struck, there is a great gouge gone
from the wall for the soldier's long knife passed

50

through Crazy Horse and lodged there till he withdrew it; I am told that men with skin like yours gaze at that gouge, and laugh and joke and say — there stood a good Indian, a dead Indian . . . My good friend Crazy Horse of the Oglala.

WALSH:

. . . Aren't things sometimes done in your name? Things you do not wish? It can be that way with white men too. I am your friend.

SITTING BULL:

I have no white friends.

WALSH:

For Christ's sake, forget the colour of our skin! If you've got no more to say than that, let's all line up and have it out! To hell with it! Is that what you want?

SITTING BULL:

Red men choke and die on white men's words!

WALSH:

When have my actions betrayed my words? I came here to speak to you as a man, and I expect the same from you! What's past is past. Crazy Horse is dead, but others live, and you and I are here to talk of them!

People are coming from the White Father in Washington. I ask you to see them. If you don't want to return with them, tell them so. I promise you I'll stand by you.

SITTING BULL:

Who do they send?

WALSH:

. . . General Terry.

SITTING BULL:

You ask me to see this man? The man who burnt my mother earth, and killed my friends! You tell me, see this man!

WALSH:

If you wish to negotiate a reservation here in Canada, you must make your peace with the Americans first. *Silence for a moment as WALSH and SITTING BULL stare at each other.* There's something more I have to say . . . last night two men rode into your camp.

SITTING BULL:

With news of Crazy Horse.

WALSH:

And news of something more than that, I think.

SITTING BULL:

They had a request to make of me.

WALSH:

Nez Perces, weren't they?

SITTING BULL:

Nez Perces, from the Valley of the Winding Waters.

WALSH:

The Wallowa Valley no longer belongs to them.

SITTING BULL:

A thief treaty — Chief Joseph did not sign!

WALSH:

Nevertheless the President has put aside a reservation, and the Indians must go onto it.

SITTING BULL:

What right has he to tell the Indian where he must go in his own land?

WALSH:

Is Chief Joseph trying to bring his people into Canada?

SITTING BULL:

I tell you what you already know — the Nez Perces are on the run. They have come to me. They request the Sioux to help them fight their way across the line.

WALSH:

What I do not know is your decision.

SITTING BULL:

I have not made it.

WALSH:

Then listen to me. If it can be proven that you've carried out an act of war against the Americans while camping here in Canada, your refuge will be in jeopardy.

SITTING BULL:

What could you do?

WALSH:

We could open the border, and allow the American Army in to drive you out.

SITTING BULL:

Even though you know you send us to our death?

WALSH:

We don't know that.

SITTING BULL:

As we speak, Nez Perces are rotting, their bodies full of bullet holes, their heads smashed in with gunstocks and bootheels. Would you term this a natural death?

WALSH:

You see my red coat — it represents the Queen and the Canadian government. My duty is to inform you of my government's position, and it is this . . . Armed excursions across the line — for whatever reason — will not be tolerated! *gently* I advise you to deny the Nez Perces.

SITTING BULL:

Men, women, children . . . they have travelled 1300 miles . . .

WALSH:

Another 60 and they're across the line. My government won't try to stop them, but you must not try to aid them either. They must make it on their own.

SITTING BULL:

You ask me to deny them.

WALSH:

It's for the good of your people. You can see that.

SITTING BULL:

. . . Yes . . . I can see it . . . Today is a sad day for me . . . In the past, I have risen, tomahawk in hand. I have done all the hurt to the whites that I could . . . Now you are here. My arms hang to the ground as if dead . . . I believe the Blackfoot and the Cree have judged you wisely. I will call you White Sioux and I will trust you. I will speak with General Terry . . . and I will deny the Nez Perces.

As the lights dim out on WALSH and SITTING BULL, they come up blue and cold, along with the BG sound of howling wind. The light picks out CLARENCE and McCUTCHEON bundled in great coats. A winter blizzard is blowing.

McCUTCHEON: *CLARENCE has stopped in front of him.* What is it?

54

CLARENCE:
We've lost the Major.

McCUTCHEON:
Keep goin', laddie.

CLARENCE:
We've lost the Major.

McCUTCHEON:
Here, let me.

He moves ahead of CLARENCE, and begins walking holding his hand up to shield himself from the wind. CLARENCE follows.

And we've no lost the Major . . . Come on, laddie, we'll wait for Louis here. *He and CLARENCE huddle together.*

CLARENCE:
My god, I'm cold!

The blue light picks out WALSH, SITTING BULL, and GALL as they enter in single file leaning against the storm.

McCUTCHEON: *cups his hands and calls*
Over here, sir!

WALSH: *as they approach*
Any sign of Louis?

McCUTCHEON: *shakes his head*
Are ye sure Sittin' Bull's information is correct?

WALSH looks at SITTING BULL.

SITTING BULL:
> The Longknives have surrounded the Nez Perce, but some have broken through.

WALSH:
> Well, if they're out there, Louis'll find them.

CLARENCE:
> Aren't you worried 'bout him?

McCUTCHEON:
> Ah, we've got naught to worry about Louis . . . he can look after himself.

CLARENCE:
> My god, I'm cold.

> *A noise. They turn and look out. A blue light picks out LOUIS. He makes his way towards the others. He comes to SITTING BULL and stands before him without speaking. There is a pause.*

WALSH:
> Well . . . speak up, Louis, have the Nez Perce crossed the border?

LOUIS: *speaks to SITTING BULL*
> I have found da tracks of a small number of people. Dey have few ponies and move slowly. Most are on foot . . . Dere trail is easy to follow . . . it is marked with frozen blood. Come with me.

> *SITTING BULL and GALL prepare to follow him. He speaks to WALSH.*

> Wait here. We speak to dem first. Dey will be frightened. We will bring dem back.

> *They leave.*

*Silence. McCUTCHEON moves towards WALSH
who stands at the edge of the light looking out. A
wolf howls. Silence, then the whinnying of a pony.
WALSH points.*

McCUTCHEON:
Is it them, sir?

*SITTING BULL returns without his outer robes. He
wears his leggings and breeches. He stands outside
of the circle of light, a silhouette.*

WALSH:
Sergeant. Constable. Help them!

*He nods his head briskly in the direction from which
SITTING BULL came. WALSH gives them his great
coat. They leave quickly.*

SITTING BULL: *an honest question*
How does the white man sustain himself beneath the
weight of the blood that he has shed?

*WALSH looks at SITTING BULL, and then off at
the muffled sounds of people approaching. The
light begins to flicker as if people were passing in
front of it, WALSH turns slowly looking outside the
light. There is a muffled sound of people moaning.
A blue light picks out CLARENCE as he makes his
way towards WALSH.*

CLARENCE:
Is . . . is it all right, sir? My coat. I've . . . I've given
it to . . . *indicates vaguely outside light* . . . to
. . . to a little girl and her brother. Their feet are
frozen, sir . . . Will the government mind about the
coat?

WALSH: *holding himself very erect, military*
I'll speak on your behalf, Constable.

CLARENCE:

It's just women and children . . . and a few men . . .
Most of them are . . . got wounds of one kind or
another. Chief Joseph, he's not with them. He
. . . didn't make it . . . It's only just people, people
that's been hurt! I don't see what they could have
done to deserve this — do you know what they've
done?

WALSH:

There . . . see there . . .   *He is hurriedly removing
his tunic. He has on long underwear top.*   Take this
. . . take this to the woman on the pony . . . there . . .
with the papoose on her back. Take it to her.

CLARENCE:

Yes sir.   *He moves towards the figure, freezes a ways
from her. The wind howls.*

*LOUIS stands on rim of light watching. CLARENCE
returns, moves slowly. He has the tunic.*

She doesn't need it — she's been hit in the chest. The
baby's dead. It's got a bit of blood on it . . .   *He
gives it an ineffectual wipe, more of a touch of the
blood, then looks at WALSH.*   . . . I didn't notice
till I put it 'round her that . . . she didn't need it.

*WALSH slowly takes the tunic. CLARENCE moves
away as WALSH stands holding the tunic. He extends
one arm, slowly, deliberately drops the tunic, and
looks out.*

*LOUIS steps forward, picks up the tunic, and passes
it to WALSH.*

LOUIS:

You can't just throw it away, sir. Dat's too easy.

*WALSH looks at him, takes the tunic, slowly exits
with it.*

*LOUIS goes down on one knee. SITTING BULL
steps forward slightly.*

*We hear the many voices of the Nez Perces softly
"Ay Ay" in the background as LOUIS speaks.*

My father has given me this nation
In protecting it
A hard time I have.

Friends, hardships pursue me,
Fearless of them,
I live.
My chiefs of old are gone.
Myself I shall take courage.

*The voices grow in volume. They stop simultaneously
with a second of blackout. Then the light comes up
on PRETTY PLUME and CROWFOOT, with SIT-
TING BULL in his former position.*

PRETTY PLUME:
Tatanka Yotanka!

*CROWFOOT runs towards SITTING BULL and
SITTING BULL picks him up laughing. As he swings
him in the air, PRETTY PLUME approaches him,
holds out rawhide bag which contains the sacred
stones.*

SITTING BULL:
Aha Little One! Get to work, your mother says.
Clear a spot.

CROWFOOT:
Now?

SITTING BULL:
Now.

*He sits, CROW EAGLE kneels, smoothing a spot to
lay out the sacred stones, sits back beside SITTING
BULL. PRETTY PLUME sits watching from a
distance.*

So! . . . *arranges the stones in the shape of the
medicine wheel* To the Great spirit belongs all
things. The four-legged and the two-legged — but to
the two-legged he gives the power to make live and to
destroy . . . To you, He gives the cup of living water —
Now . . . see? *indicating the circle of stones* It
makes the sacred hoop. Here is the cross within the
circle dividing it in four.

*CLARENCE appears and stops before intruding.
CLARENCE draws nearer during the following
speeches as he becomes interested.*

The Great Spirit caused everything to be in fours.
Four directions — north, east, south, west; four
divisions of time — the day, the night, the month,
the year; four parts of everything that grows — the
root, the stem, the leaves, the fruit . . . what else?

CROWFOOT:
Ahhhhh . . .

*SITTING BULL holds out his hands, palm downward,
his thumbs concealed. CROWFOOT thrusts his out
likewise.*

Four fingers on each hand . . . and . . . two arms, two
legs . . . *thrusts four limbs, laughing* Four in all!

*CLARENCE is interested and casts a furtive look at
his own hands.*

SITTING BULL: *urging CROWFOOT on*
Four things above the earth — the sun . . . the
moon . . .

CROWFOOT:
The sky, the stars!

SITTING BULL: *smiles and nods at CROWFOOT*
Good. All of the universe is enclosed and revealed in
the sacred circle. *tracing it* Do you see how the
Sun Dance is a sacred hoop, and the Sun Dance pole,
the sacred centre? What else?

CLARENCE: *caught up, breaks in*
The tipi!

SITTING BULL looks at him.

Like, it's a circle too and . . . the fire . . . that's the
centre.

*He shifts nervously, bumps one of the stones, picks it
up, is not sure where it goes, and gives it to SITTING
BULL.*

SITTING BULL: *holds up the stone*
This is a sacred stone. See how round it is. Everything the Great Spirit does is done in a circle. The
sun and moon are round — they come and go forth
in a circle. The white man says the earth is round,
and so are all the stars. What else?

CROWFOOT:
Birds make their nests round!

WALSH enters quietly.

SITTING BULL:
The winds whirl, the seasons form a great circle, and
when we, the Sioux, meet as a Nation, we set our
tipis so . . . *describes an arc with the hand holding
the stone* The Nation's Hoop!

*He replaces the stone in position. Pauses for a
moment, then looks at WALSH.*

Do you come to speak with me?

WALSH:

I want to thank you for seeing the Americans today.

*SITTING BULL dismisses PRETTY PLUME and
CROWFOOT. WALSH dismisses CLARENCE.*

I've been talking to General Terry. *pause*

*SITTING BULL makes no comment forcing him to
continue.*

I believe him to be a gentlemen, a man of his word.
another pause Do you realize what he's promised
should you return across the line? A reservation,
food and supplies for your people, and a complete
amnesty! . . . No one will be punished or go to jail
for acts of war committed against the government.
All that will be forgiven and forgotten.

SITTING BULL:

Forgotten . . . When I was a boy, the Sioux owned
the world — the sun rose and set on their land. They
sent 10,000 men to battle. Where are those warriors
now? Who slew them? Where are our lands? Who
owns them? Tell me — What law have I broken? Is
it wrong for me to love my own? Is it wicked for me
because my skin is red? Because I am a Sioux, because I was born where my fathers lived, because I
would die for my people and my country?

This white man would "forgive" me — and while he
talks to me of forgiveness, what do his people say to
yours? "Seize their guns and horses! Drive them
back across the line! The more we kill this year, the
less we have to kill next year!" Is it not true?

SITTING BULL stares at WALSH who cannot deny that this is the strategy put forward by some.

You are a white man. The god whose son you killed must love you and your people well for he has rewarded you with many gifts . . . and tools . . . and . . . *indicating with his hand their uniforms, guns, etc.* all this. I am told wisdom is yours as well . . . Advise me now, White Sioux. Tell me what is best for my people. I will follow your advice, and the burden of it will be on your shoulders . . .

WALSH doesn't answer.

Shall I lead my people into the arms of the Long-knives? Will they protect us as "feathers do a bird"? . . . Look inside your heart! You have a heart. I saw it the night the Nez Perces crossed the line. What does your heart say?

WALSH: *agitated*
You know if you refuse this offer, there'll be nothing for you here. My government says they won't feed you or give you reservations.

SITTING BULL:
Is your advice then to return with the Americans?

WALSH:
My advice! . . . is . . . to consider . . . to consider the consequences of your actions. That is my advice.

SITTING BULL:
What does that mean?

WALSH:
It means — if you stay — you're dependent on the buffalo, and when they go, as they are surely going, we won't care for you as we do our own Indians.

Now if you go with General Terry, he has given his word that you won't be mistreated or — *stops himself from saying "killed"* You will be fed and clothed.

SITTING BULL:
Would you choose to live as you advise me to do?

WALSH:
I don't advise you to do this! I . . . merely state your choices.

SITTING BULL:
I know many who took the white man's promise . . . Bear Ribs, White Antelope, Iron Shield, Black Kettle, Stirring Bear . . . Crazy Horse. I would ask their guidance — but all of them are dead.

WALSH:
You . . . make your point.

SITTING BULL: *dropping all pretense of asking for advice*
Let us speak clearly to each other — if the President in Washington can say "come, you are safe here" — and then change his mind and let the Longknives kill us . . . Can it not work the other way too? *looks intently at WALSH* Cannot the Great White Mother say "no food or reservations" — but then reconsider? Our Brothers, the Santee Sioux from across the line . . .

WALSH:
. . . have been given a reservation in Manitoba. Quite right.

SITTING BULL: *opening up to WALSH with his secret fear*
I believe the Americans are only waiting to get us all together, and then they will slaughter us; that is what I believe.

WALSH: *thinks, decides*
Right! . . . Well now, I've delivered my government's message to which your reply is . . .

SITTING BULL:
The Sioux are self-sufficient!

WALSH:
Mn . . . and I shall give your final decision to General Terry, that is . . .

SITTING BULL: *joking*
Tell him he can take it easy on the way back. The Sioux only fight with men.

WALSH: *smiles*
I was thinking of something a bit more formal.

SITTING BULL: *begins by playing the role a bit*
He came here to tell us lies, but we don't want to hear them. I intend to stay here . . . and to raise my people in this country.

The lights begin to fade, SITTING BULL leaves. WALSH looks after him for a moment, then goes to leave.

LOUIS: *speaks from shadows*
Major!

WALSH stops, looks at him.

Does da Major know what month dis is?

WALSH:
The month when the green grass comes up.

LOUIS: *no humour*
Major damn good pupil.

WALSH: *almost abruptly*
Louis damn good teacher. *turns to go*

LOUIS: *moves towards WALSH*
Louis "request" permission to speak to da Major.

WALSH: *a trace of irritation*
Here and now?

LOUIS:
Last fall, crossin' da Milk River, da Major's horse step in dat sink hole, and Louis, he grab da Major and pull 'im out . . .

WALSH nods.

. . . Da other year, when Louis hear all kind of big story 'bout da 'ssiniboin makin' trouble — Louis tell da Major — even t'ough dat 'ssiniboin is son of good friend of Louis' mother . . .

WALSH:
The Major is in your debt.

LOUIS:
And some of Louis' mother's people don't speak to him no more, but dis don't matter, for Louis trust da Major to do da right thing . . . Dis is da month when da green grass come up, da Moon of Makin' Fat; dis is spring . . . can da Major make da spring come for da Sioux? What can you do for Sittin' Bull?

WALSH:
Everything within my power.

LOUIS:
How much is dat?

WALSH:
Do you insult me, Louis, or my government?

LOUIS:

Louis choose to trust, but da Indian can do nothin'
else but trust. Trust. Or die . . . Sometime trust *and*
die . . . Can da Major make da spring come for da
Sioux?

WALSH:

You trust in me, and I trust in those above me, quite
simple, eh? Now let's get on . . . *goes to leave*

LOUIS:

Da Indian say he would trust da Great White Mother
more if she did not have so many bald-headed thieves
workin' for her!

WALSH: *stops, turns, angry*

The Sioux have a case, a strong case, and I shall
present it!

LOUIS: *softly*

Who stands behind you dere?

WALSH:

Honourable men!

LOUIS spits.

BLACKOUT

Act Two

Lights come up on HARRY, CLARENCE, LOUIS and McCUTCHEON. Lights are punctuated by LOUIS' throwing of knife into the floor of the stage. A dull thud. LOUIS sits with his rifle unslung. McCUTCHEON sits cleaning his saddle. CLARENCE is attempting to thread a needle. As HARRY watches the three of them. McCUTCHEON leans over, picks the needle from CLARENCE, threads it efficiently, and passes it back. CLARENCE looks up at him.

CLARENCE:
Thanks . . .   *begins mending a sock*

HARRY and McCUTCHEON exchange a look of amusement.

HARRY:
Sewin' detail, eh?   *begins to roll a cigarette as he watches CLARENCE*

CLARENCE: *intent on sewing*
Yeah . . . I wish me mum were here . . .

McCUTCHEON tosses HARRY a match for his cigarette.

This ain't my idea of police work.

McCUTCHEON:
Ah laddie, your poor wee face would have been wet with tears for your mum if ye'd been with the Force on our march west in '73. I don't know what ye'd have called that.

HARRY: *settling down to watch everyone work*
It weren't the Mounted Police then, Clarence, it were the Dismounted Police — Lost practically every horse they had. *laughs*

McCUTCHEON:
Aye, a man with the best will in the world couldn't call it the Force's finest hour.

LOUIS:
Dey didn't have Louis with dem. Dey need a good scout.

McCUTCHEON:
I never saw so many bugs — black flies so thick they clogged your nose so ye couldn't draw breath, and every man from the Colonel down infected with fleas. It's a lovely time y're havin' laddie, ye don't appreciate it.

CLARENCE:
Yeah . . . well . . . me mum always mended my things at home.

HARRY:

Jesus Christ Clarence, you had a good thing there, boy, your mum waitin' on you hand an foot. What'd you want to go and join up for? You could have had it easy in the east.

CLARENCE:

My dad was a soldier.

HARRY:

You don't say.

CLARENCE:

Yup. Half-pay officer, served in the Crimean, he did . . . And after that, he and me mum, they come out to Upper Canada in '60. First winter out, my dad, he died . . . I can't hardly remember him, but my mum, she used to tell me 'bout him bein' a soldier and all . . . It was hard goin' for us . . . I think me mum was the real soldier . . .

McCUTCHEON:

No brothers or sisters, laddie?

CLARENCE:

Nope . . . Mum's all alone back east.

HARRY:

You ain't told us why you joined.

CLARENCE:

Well . . . me mum, she said I was a man like my dad . . . and I had to find my own place, couldn't sit in Glengarry growin' potatoes, and tendin' to her. And she was right . . . I got to thinking . . .

HARRY:

Yeah?

CLARENCE:

You all'd laugh.

HARRY:
No, we wouldn't.

CLARENCE:
Well, I got to thinkin', out here in the territories, that was where everything was happenin', the Indian Wars, and Openin' the West, and Wild Bill Hickcock sittin' on the biggest, blackest horse you every saw! *He looks at HARRY, McCUTCHEON, and LOUIS, who regard him seriously.* I wanted to do what was right, and excitin', and . . . and make me mum proud of me.

McCUTCHEON looks out at the horizon and sniffs.

HARRY:
How do you figure it's turned out?

CLARENCE:
I guess she's proud of me . . . not so excitin' as I thought it'd be . . . and as far as what's right goes — that don't seem to come into it . . .

McCUTCHEON:
What's that in the air, Louis? Smoke?

LOUIS:
Lotta smoke . . . dere goin' be more.

CLARENCE:
I don't smell nothin'.

HARRY:
Hell, Clarence, you won't smell it till tomorrow or next day — The Sergeant here, he smell it today, and Louis. *smiling at LOUIS* When'd you smell it, Louis?

LOUIS: *holds up two fingers*
Two day ago.

CLARENCE:
What's it from?

LOUIS:
Da 'mericans fire da border.

CLARENCE: *curious*
What?

LOUIS:
'Merican soldiers, da Longknives, dey set fires all
'long da border, two or three hundred mile long every
ten mile or so.

CLARENCE: *to McCUTCHEON*
What's he sayin'? That don't make sense, Louis.

LOUIS:
Make a lotta sense.

HARRY:
It's this way, Clarence. The buffalo across the line
start movin' north, so the soldiers burn all along the
border — the buffalo turn back, and then the American government don't have to feed the reservation
Indians.

CLARENCE looks at him blankly.

They're supposed to hunt and feed themselves!

CLARENCE:
Well, what about *our* Indians?

LOUIS: *surprised*
You got some Indians?

CLARENCE:
You know what I mean.

LOUIS ignores him and looks at gun.

O.K. What about *the* Indians livin' on the Canadian side of the line.

LOUIS:
What about dem?

CLARENCE:
What're they supposed to do?

HARRY:
Eat grass.

CLARENCE: *angry*
I don't believe you! Besides I don't smell nothin'.
It's all a lie. There's no smoke in the air!
Do you smell smoke, Sergeant?

McCUTCHEON:
Look at that haze over the hills, laddie.

CLARENCE:
That's a heat haze . . . from the sun.

HARRY:
You think so, eh?

CLARENCE:
Well, I don't believe it! It ain't fair! And even if it
was true, and there weren't no buffalo, and nothin'
for them to eat, well then, the Canadian government,
it'd send out food for them. It's got a responsibility!

LOUIS: *shrugs*
Maybeso.

HARRY:
So the Canadian government feeds its own Indians . . .
Who's gonna feed the Sioux?

CLARENCE:
They're people, aren't they?

McCUTCHEON, HARRY, and LOUIS look at him.

You don't let people starve to death, do you? Just cause you wish they'd move someplace else, you don't let people starve! You can't do things like that. You can't do things like that!

He stares at HARRY, McCUTCHEON, and LOUIS. They all freeze. HARRY pulls document out and reads from it as light slowly dims.

HARRY:
MacDonald reports that though the Sioux have behaved themselves remarkably well since crossing into Canada, their presence in the North West Territories has been attended by serious consequences. The buffalo are rapidly diminishing and the advent of so large a body of foreign Indians has precipitated their diminution. The Sioux are already feeling the hardship and are hard pressed to avert danger and suffering from famine.

The light blacks out. About four bars of calliope music. Lights come up on MARY sitting embroidering and on WALSH a distance away from her. The music fades as WALSH speaks.

WALSH:
My . . . dearest . . . Mary . . . My dearest Mary.

MARY:
Jim.

WALSH:
Two letters came in today, along with a load of winter supplies. I don't know which I was happier to see.

MARY:

The girls are fine; it's been so long since they've
seen you.

WALSH:

. . . You'll think I've got a touch of prairie fever but
the solitude here, the emptiness of these Great Plains,
fills me with a sense of timelessness.

MARY:

Both send their love.

WALSH:

Remember the day we picnicked on the river? Cora
plump and placid on the blanket, little Mary showing
me her hands stained with the juice of flowers . . .
and you bent over the basket, your hair hanging loose
and laughing . . . you look 18.

MARY:

I hope you're looking after yourself. *laughs* How
often do I say that?

WALSH:

You're not to worry about my health. McCutcheon's
like a mother hen.

MARY:

Here in the east we're always hearing grand tales of
Major Walsh, how he's subdued the Sioux and Sitting
Bull.

WALSH:

The Sioux — Common sense, honesty, and humanity.

MARY:

The treachery.

WALSH:
> Ah Mary, we call our actions strategy or tactics; we call theirs treachery . . . My god, if I could only show you what I see every day — the buffalo are gone, vanished; like frost at dawn, one minute here, the next — nowhere. In the fall, the Sioux were hungry. Now it's winter, and they starve.

MARY:
> After church supper, the choir sang.

WALSH:
> Sickness, plain suffering, kills them like flies. Most of their ponies are dead, and their rotting carcasses are cut up for food . . . Yes, they're starving and destitute, yet they endure. They share what little they have, and they observe the law — god damn it, they'd be a credit to any community . . . Ottawa has not acknowledged my recommendations . . .

MARY: *smiling*
> You always say don't worry.

WALSH:
> I wonder if Dewdney has even forwarded them.

MARY:
> But of course I worry. It's natural to worry. *laughing* Yesterday I found another gray hair. You won't know me when you return.

WALSH:
> I try to understand the government's viewpoint — Jesus Christ, I'm no raw recruit! One thing I know, across the line there's been gross and continual mismanagement of the Sioux. An able and brilliant people have been crushed, held down, moved from place to place, cheated and lied to — And now they hold on here in Canada, the remnants of a proud race, and they ask for some sort of justice — which is what I thought I swore an oath to serve!

MARY: *distant — light begins to fade*
Your "little" Mary's soon to be thirteen — don't forget her birthday, will you?

WALSH:
We carried great bouquets of flowers home that day. *looks down at his hands* . . . She's not thirteen . . .

MARY:
Cora's getting thin.

WALSH:
Cora red and bawling, and you with your hair spread on the pillow, smiling and offering me your hand . . .

Light is out on MARY — a spot on WALSH's figure.

The girls still babies, you 18 in the east . . . suspended in amber . . . while I grow old in the west . . .

McCUTCHEON:
Colonel MacLeod to see you, sir.

WALSH:
MacLeod? Send him on in.

MacLEOD. WALSH springs up to greet him sincerely. Both are original members of the Force and friends.

Welcome to the Fort, Colonel. Pleasant journey, I trust?

MacLEOD:
Not bad, Major, not bad . . . You're looking well.

McCUTCHEON:
Is there anything else, sir?

WALSH:
> No, McCutcheon. Stand down.

McCUTCHEON leaves.

MacLEOD:
> To tell the truth, Jim you look like death. What the hell have you been up to?

WALSH:
> If you think I look bad, you should see the horses.

MacLEOD:
> That so?

WALSH:
> It's been a hard winter.

MacLEOD: *clipping end of cigar*
> Seems to be the case right across the West.

WALSH gets out flask, looks at MacLEOD who nods "yes" to a drink.

WALSH:
> Are you doing the tour early? The boys at Fort Walsh are always on their toes. It'll be a . . .

MacLEOD:
> Nothing like that.

WALSH: *stiffens somewhat*
> Do you bring news for the Sioux?

MacLEOD:
> Sit down, Jim. I'd like a wee informal talk with you.

WALSH:
> Well now, you've caught my interest. *sits* What is it?

Pause as MacLEOD examines the end of his cigar.
He looks up at WALSH. Pause.

MacLEOD:
Soooo . . . horses had a bad winter, eh?

WALSH:
What the hell are you here for?

MacLEOD: *putting letter on desk*
Recognize that?

WALSH: *glances at letter, drops it back on the desk*
I usually recognize my own correspondence. It's a
letter I sent Frank Mills at Fort Benton across the
line. Why're you dropping it on my desk like a hot
potato?

MacLEOD:
I'd be most surprised to hear that you're unaware of
the proper channels one must go through when making
a suggestion of the nature contained in this letter.

WALSH:
My note to Frank Mills suggests an exchange of stolen
horses. American horses stolen by Canadian Indians
to be exchanged for Canadian horses stolen by American Indians . . . hardly an international incident.

MacLEOD:
And what is the proper channel through which we
should negotiate an arrangement like this?

WALSH:
The proper channel? Yes, sir. I should send a
recommendation to my commanding officer, Colonel
MacLeod — if he decides to act on it, he will send a
recommendation to Ottawa — if it ever reaches the
Prime Minister's office and he decides to act on it, he
will send a recommendation to London — it is
possible that London will send it to Washington, and

Washington to Mills' commanding officer, and God
willing and the mails providing, Mills will receive a
recommendation concerning the exchange of stolen
horses. Jesus Christ, man! That's 6,000 miles and
the Lord knows how many bureaucratic bunglers.
Frank Mills is 60 miles to the south of me. Are you
trying to tell me that you object to my simplifying
matters?

MacLEOD:
It's not my objecting to it — Mills apparently objects
to it.

WALSH:
What the hell do you mean by that?

MacLEOD:
He forwarded your "note" to Fort Robson. To make
a long story short, the President has sent a formal
protest to the Queen regarding the high-handed
methods of a certain officer of the Force serving the
Canadian West . . .

WALSH:
Son-of-a-bitch! *to himself* The next god damn
American horse the boys bring in, I'll have it shot.

MacLEOD:
You realize as well as I do that this is only the tip of
the iceberg.

WALSH: *back to MacLEOD*
Where are you now, Colonel — back on the cold
winter again?

MacLEOD:
I'm talking about the real reason for the American
protest against your behaviour. I'm talking about
Sitting Bull and the Sioux.

WALSH: *stiffens, more formal*
I'm afraid I don't follow you, sir.

MacLEOD:
Jim, the Americans believe, and they have convinced
the Prime Minister, that you are privately urging
Sitting Bull to remain in Canada, while publicly
stating that he must leave.

WALSH:
Which indicates how little they know of Sitting Bull.
When his mind's made up, no man can sway him.

MacLEOD:
Not even his friends?

WALSH:
He has no white friends.

MacLEOD:
He calls you White Sioux. What is that supposed to
mean?

WALSH:
We have an understanding.

MacLEOD:
Oh? Which means?

WALSH:
We understand each other.

MacLEOD: *tapping letter*
The protest over this is an attempt to discredit you
and it all leads back to the Sioux. You're close to
that old war horse. Persuade him to return across
the line. God damn it, he's a thorn in our flesh. We
can't discuss a bloody thing with the Americans without they bring it up!

WALSH:

What up?

MacLEOD:

Our giving sanctuary to those responsible for the
Custer massacre. They talk of nothing else.

WALSH:

Custer was responsible for the death of himself and
his men! For Christ's sake, speak the truth!

MacLEOD:

I'm not here to argue with you. I'm here as a friend.

WALSH:

I've had my orders and I've followed them.

MacLEOD:

I'm asking you to do more than that . . . He trusts
you.

WALSH:

Because he knows I won't deceive him.

MACLEOD:

He'll listen to you.

WALSH:

Because he trusts me, and he knows I won't deceive
him!

MacLEOD: *softly*

How am I asking you to deceive him? *pause* The
Sioux have no future here in Canada.

WALSH:

Tell me something. It was you, as Commissioner of
the North West Mounted Police, who impressed upon
me that a part of my duty, no less important than
the policing of this area, was the accurate observation
and recording of events, no matter how minute. Such
a report to be sent monthly, along with my recommendations for government policy.

MacLEOD:

Quite correct.

WALSH:

Then why the hell is nothing acted upon?

MacLEOD:

Did you not receive two stallions come in with Harry
to sire your mares? Are you not now in the act of
digging a new well?

WALSH:

I'm not talking about domestic trivia! I don't need a
statement from the god damn Prime Minister to under-
take a new well!

MacLEOD:

Ah, but you do, Jim.

WALSH:

My men are not in the act of digging a new well — my
men *dug* a new well two months before permission
was granted! The entire fort would have been down
with typhoid or dead of thirst had I waited for
word from Ottawa.

MacLEOD sighs and shakes his head.

What about my recommendations concerning the
Indians?

MacLEOD:
>What about them?

WALSH:
>The Sioux have as much legal right to a reservation here, as the Santee Sioux had in Manitoba.

MacLEOD:
>The Santee Sioux did not kill Custer.

WALSH:
>They killed over 600 white settlers in Minnesota who were not engaged in an act of war against them. Why are my recommendations not acted upon?

MacLEOD:
>Out here you don't see the whole picture. There're other considerations.

WALSH:
>My recommendations are ignored! I may as well post them in the privy!

MacLEOD:
>You play chess — sometimes a pawn is sacrificed on one side of the board to gain an advantage on the other.

WALSH: *disbelief*
>I am a pawn?

MacLEOD:
>No, no, Jim, not you — it might be possible to consider Sitting Bull and the Sioux as pawns.

WALSH:
>What are the advantages to be gained from this . . . this sacrifice?

MacLEOD:

We can't know that, can we? That's the kind of weighty decision the Prime Minister and London must contend with.

WALSH:

I demand to know what advantage is to be gained!

MacLEOD:

The Prime Minister is not responsible to you, Jim!

WALSH:

God damn it, he is! If I carry out his orders, he is responsible to me!

MacLEOD:

You're talking nonsense! An army that operated like that couldn't navigate its way across a playing field! And you know it!

WALSH:

What do you think happens when I take off this tunic? At night, in my quarters, what do you think happens to me?

MacLEOD:

Jim —

WALSH:

Do you think McCutcheon hangs me up from some god damn wooden peg with all my strings dangling? Is that what you think happens? Do you think I'm a puppet? Manipulate me right and anything is possible. I'm a person, I exist. I think and feel! And I will not allow you to do this to me.

MacLEOD: *softly*

To do what to you? . . . I merely ask you to use your position with Sitting Bull to convince him to leave the country in the best interests of his people.

WALSH:

I've had my orders and I've followed them . . .

MacLEOD:

You're tired, Jim.

WALSH:

Ask my men if I am tired. No one at this post rises earlier or is to bed later. Fatigue is unknown to me.

MacLEOD:

You work yourself too hard.

WALSH:

I have a job and I do it.

MacLEOD:

It's a long time since you've been home.

WALSH:

Home? . . . I don't request a leave of absence, Colonel . . . Shall we get on with the business at hand?

MacLEOD:

I have two dispatches from the Prime Minister. The first concerns the Sioux.

WALSH:

What is it?

MacLEOD:

You are to see that no foodstuffs, clothing, ammunition or supplies is given them, if they do not possess the money to pay for them.

WALSH:

They have no money.

MacLEOD:

> It has been brought to the attention of the Prime Minister that certain settlers as well as members of the Force itself have been supplying the Sioux with various odds and ends of food and clothing. This must stop at once.

WALSH:

> Yes, sir.

MacLEOD:

> The Prime Minister feels that whereas common sense has not prevailed upon the Sioux — hunger will.
> *He looks at WALSH for a moment, then back to his dispatch.* My second dispatch concerns your ill-advised note to Major Mills.

WALSH:

> Yes, sir.

MacLEOD:

> An apology is to be written couched in the appropriate words stating that you humbly beg the American government's pardon for overstepping the limits of your authority. *pause* Is that understood?

WALSH:

> I . . .

MacLEOD:

> If you find yourself unable to do this, it is my sad duty to ask for your resignation.

WALSH:

> How well you know your men.

MacLEOD:

> I pride myself on that.

WALSH:
They say one's strongest instinct is self-preservation — and I've made the Force my life . . . To whom do I send this letter?

MacLEOD:
To your commanding officer, myself, naturally.

WALSH:
Ah, yes.

MacLEOD:
I'll see that it's forwarded to Ottawa . . . Well, Jim, how about a walk around the post before bed. Bit of pleasure after a surfeit of business.

WALSH:
McCutcheon! . . . Sorry, Colonel, I've a few things to attend to. McCutcheon will see you to your quarters.

McCUTCHEON enters.

Good night, sir.

MacLEOD:
Good night, Jim.

WALSH stands rigid until McCUTCHEON and MacLEOD exit. He pours himself another drink. He walks outside the office, stands looking out at the prairies, with the flask in his hand. We hear someone whistling "Garryowen".

WALSH: *listens, then*
That you, Harry?

HARRY:
You give me a start there, Major. I didn't expect to see nobody up at this time of night.

WALSH drinks and extends flask to HARRY.

Don't mind if I do.   *takes drink, retains flask*
I been up visitin' with Sittin' Bull. Always a dry
night when you visit with the old man. Lots of
tobacco, but no booze.

WALSH:
Fraternizing, eh?

HARRY:
Oh no, nothin' like that. Just chewin' the fat.
pause   Hear MacLeod come in today . . . bit early,
ain't he?   *pause*   Is he here for the tour?

WALSH: *brings his attention back to HARRY*
. . . No, no, he isn't.

HARRY:
O-fficial business, eh? O-fficial business.

WALSH:
Do you know Brockville, Harry?

HARRY:
Can't say as I do . . .

WALSH:
Pretty town . . . trees. Shade in the summer time . . .
cool and green.

HARRY:
Hell of a change from this place I reckon.

WALSH:
My wife lives in Brockville . . . and my two girls.

HARRY:
Ain't got a son?

WALSH:

> No. No son . . . just as well . . . no son. Pretty place
> though.

HARRY:

> What the hell. Have another drink, Major. *passes
> flask to him*

WALSH: *drinks, passes it back to HARRY*
> I've always been a man of principles, Harry. I've
> always thought of myself as a man of principle . . .
> Honour, truth, the lot . . . They're just words, Harry.
> They don't exist. I gave my life to them and they
> don't exist.

> *HARRY stares at WALSH.*

HARRY: *uneasy*
> You should get to bed, Major. It ain't night, it's
> mornin'.

WALSH: *smiles*
> Fatigue is unknown to me.

> *HARRY smiles back, feeling he's back on more
> familiar ground.*

HARRY:

> That's a fact, sir. That's a fact. Ain't never knowed
> you to be tired.

> *WALSH reaches for the flask, drinks, gives it back to
> HARRY.*

WALSH:

> You were up visiting the Sioux, were you?

HARRY:

> Yessireee. Course they knowed MacLeod's come in.
> Naturally they's wonderin' if it means anythin' for
> them.

WALSH:

Oh yes, I should say it does.

HARRY:

Good news?

WALSH:

The Sioux have no future here in Canada.

HARRY:

They sure as hell don't have none south of the line.

WALSH:

The government's concern stops at the border.

HARRY:

Major, you get yourself too het up.

WALSH:

I see . . . larger issues at stake.

HARRY:

Don't see what's a larger issue than a man's life . . .
No Injun agent's gonna put up with Sittin' Bull.

WALSH:

You think not?

HARRY:

They'll kill him off. Only smart thing to do, ain't
it?

WALSH:

And how do you feel about that?

HARRY:

Ain't nothin' I can do. . . . Good night, Major.

WALSH stares at HARRY as HARRY exits. WALSH follows as PRETTY PLUME enters with pipe, followed by CROWFOOT. She sings:

Little One, little one,
Loved by everyone.
Little One speaks sweet words to everyone
That is why, that is why
Little One is loved by everyone.

CROWFOOT puts his head in her lap in semi-darkness outside scene.

CLARENCE sneaks furtively into light, carrying a small knapsack.

CLARENCE: *whispers*
Pssssttt! . . . Little One! . . . Little One!

SITTING BULL: *from shadows*
Is it my son you seek?

CLARENCE: *frightened, starts*
Oh! . . . Ah . . . yes sir, I was just . . . a . . . *hastily tries to conceal the knapsack behind him* . . . I was just . . . lookin' for your little boy.

SITTING BULL comes into light. He looks older and his face is drawn.

SITTING BULL:
You are the young man who rides out with White Sioux . . . Is he with you?

CLARENCE:
Ah well, no sir, I . . . come by myself . . . I brought . . . *quickly thrusts knapsack at SITTING BULL* ah . . . *nods at sack* . . . some things from the mess, sir. I'd like the little boy to have them .

SITTING BULL: *takes sack, nods his thanks*
You have a good heart . . . I have little to offer you in return . . . *sees pipe, checks his tobacco pouch, smiles* Come! Have a pipe with me! *sits and motions CLARENCE down*

CLARENCE:
Well, I . . . don't know if I should.

SITTING BULL:
Sit!

CLARENCE sits in silence as SITTING BULL prepares pipe and passes it to him. Silence as they smoke a bit.

. . . Times are bad. They say there are still buffalo south of the line, but if we go to hunt them, the bluecoats will kill us. *laughs drily* It hardly matters as our ponies are too weak to carry us there in the first place. But my heart grows weak and trembles when I hear the little children cry for food . . . It is a hard thing. *smiles at CLARENCE* And you feel that way too. See? We are not so much different.

CLARENCE:
Don't you think, maybe, you could think about goin' back? Everybody hungry and everythin'. Is it worth it?

SITTING BULL:
Across the line, on the reservations, they are starving too. We hear these things and so must your people.

CLARENCE nods.

The white man is afraid to kill us outright, but he knows if he kills the buffalo, we must soon follow . . . I myself do not understand why you should wish this on us.

CLARENCE:
I don't wish nothin' like that.

SITTING BULL:
And I think, if you give me nothing, and you will not let me go where I can get something for myself, what is there? I would rather die fighting, than die of starvation.

CLARENCE: *uneasy*
You'd just all get killed that way.

SITTING BULL:
Yes. That is the warrior's way out — but I am not only a warrior. I must think of *all* my people. I must think of the ones here now, and the ones that come after . . . what is best for them . . . I know we must change.

CLARENCE:
Yeah. I guess that's it.

SITTING BULL:
Sometimes one has something of value. Dogs come and spoil it for you, yet you do not wish to see it destroyed . . . I am of the Hunkpapa Sioux of the Prairie, and the Prairie will provide for me. When the buffalo are gone, my children will hunt mice; when my horse falls, I shall chase gopher; and when there is nothing else, we shall dig and eat roots . . . And I pray to the Great Spirit that the White Mother gives the thought to her children that I give to mine.

We hear WALSH harshly laughing, and the lights dim on SITTING BULL and CLARENCE. They come up on WALSH seated looking at letter. He rips it in half. McCUTCHEON is going through some papers. McCUTCHEON concentrates on his business. He knows what's coming and is preparing himself for it.

WALSH:

    Why is nothing simple in this life? It all seems per-
fectly simple to me. Why do people make it complex?
The simplest thing, complex . . . McCutcheon! Are
you listening to me?!

McCUTCHEON:

    Aye sir.

WALSH:

    Well then, why is everything so god damn complex?

McCUTCHEON:

    I don't know, sir.

WALSH: *leaps up and begins to pace*

    I write a report, a perfectly simple report, in which
I state that our Indians as well as the Sioux are suffering severe deprivation because of the extinction of
the buffalo. Is that simple or is that not?

McCUTCHEON:

    Perfectly simple, sir.

WALSH:

    Right! . . . And if we do not make a sincere and
wholehearted effort to aid these Indians, we can
expect trouble necessitating a build-up in troops,
horses, and supplies, plus the possibility of loss of
life as well as property . . . And what is the government's reply to this?

McCUTCHEON:

    I don't know, sir.

WALSH: *explodes*

    The son-of-a-bitch's going to send me more men!
And to top it all off, I'll probably get a recommendation for my foresight!

CLARENCE enters with papers. WALSH takes them.

Were you in court yesterday?

CLARENCE:
No sir.

WALSH:
I sat in judgement yesterday. I sat in judgement of a Sioux, his wife and child were starving. He slaughtered a cow belonging to a settler, and then . . . *laughs*

CLARENCE looks nervously, quickly, to McCUTCHEON, and back to WALSH.

. . . Do you know what the damn fool did?

CLARENCE:
No sir, I . . .

WALSH:
He took his horse, his only horse, told the settler what had happened, and offered the horse in payment. The settler refused, and pressed charges. And yesterday I sentenced that Sioux to 6 months imprisonment, and fined him 20 dollars. For that is the law! But where's the justice in it?

LOUIS enters. WALSH whirls on him barks out.

What is it?!

Quick look between LOUIS and McCUTCHEON.

For god's sake, man, did you come in here to gape. Speak up!

LOUIS:
Sittin' Bull's outside.

*WALSH stares at LOUIS for a moment. He becomes
very calm, sits in a chair, picks up a pencil, begins to
examine it.*

WALSH:
And why is Sitting Bull's geographical location
supposed to be of interest to me?

LOUIS:
He wants to see you.

WALSH:
I'm busy.

LOUIS: *stares hard at WALSH*
I sent him on in!   *turns to go*

WALSH:
Louis!   *LOUIS stops.*   Just . . . give me a minute.

*LOUIS exits. WALSH puts pencil down, looks at
McCUTCHEON and CLARENCE, turns around and
does up the top button on his tunic. His shoulders
stiffen. SITTING BULL enters. WALSH has his
back towards him. LOUIS follows SITTING BULL
in. SITTING BULL has a ragged blanket wrapped
round him. He looks gaunt, not well, although his
personal magnetism is still evident. He stops, looking
at WALSH's back.*

SITTING BULL:
White Sioux . . .

WALSH: *without turning*
Yes.

SITTING BULL:
I wish to speak with you.

WALSH: *turns, looks at him*
I'm listening.

98

SITTING BULL:
Have you had news from the Great White Mother?

WALSH:
My news is always the same. No reservations, no food, no clothing, no supplies.

SITTING BULL:
I wish you to send the Great White Mother a special message from Sitting Bull.

WALSH:
What is it?

SITTING BULL:
Tell her . . . once I was strong and brave; my people had hearts of iron. But now my women are sick, my children are freezing, and I have thrown my war paint to the wind. The suffering of my people has made my heart weak, and I have placed nothing in the way of those who wished to return across the line. Many have done so. We who remain desire a home. For three years we have been in the White Mother's land, we have obeyed her laws, and we have kept the peace . . . I beg the White Mother to . . . to . . .

WALSH:
Go on.

SITTING BULL:
. . . to have . . . pity . . . on us.

WALSH:
Right! Well then . . . I'll see that this goes off . . .

SITTING BULL makes no move to leave.

Is there anything else?

SITTING BULL: *gazes at WALSH*
. . . White Sioux . . .

WALSH:
   Yes?

SITTING BULL: *speaks slowly with effort*
   I find it necessary . . . to make a request . . .

   WALSH stares at him.

   . . . a request . . . for . . . provisions for my people.
   We have nothing.

WALSH: *brusquely*
   Your provisions wait for you across the line. If you
   want provisions, go there for them.

SITTING BULL:
   We hear you have a quantity of flour and I have come
   to ask you for it.

WALSH:
   If you wish to do business, you do it at the trading
   post.

   *SITTING BULL takes off his ragged blanket. He
   holds out the blanket to WALSH. WALSH begins to
   breathe heavily as he struggles to retain control of
   himself.*

   I have appealed to the Great White Mother, and the
   Great White Mother says, "No".

SITTING BULL:
   I ask for only a little.

WALSH: *explodes*
   And I can give you nothing! God knows I've done
   my damndest and nothing's changed. Do you hear
   that? Nothing's changed! Cross the line if you're
   so hungry, but don't for christ's sake come begging
   food from me!

SITTING BULL: *straightens up*
You are speaking to the Head of the Sioux Nation!

WALSH:
I don't give a god damn who you are! Get the hell out!

SITTING BULL goes for the knife in his belt. WALSH grabs him by the arm, twists it up and throws him to the floor. As SITTING BULL goes to get up WALSH places his foot in the middle of SITTING BULL's back and shoves, sending him sprawling. WALSH places his foot on SITTING BULL's back.

CLARENCE: *screams*
Noooo!

McCUTCHEON grabs CLARENCE — everyone freezes for a moment.

WALSH: *strained*
McCutcheon, Underhill, go out and alert the boys in case of trouble. Throw a couple of poles across the road.

McCUTCHEON:
Yes sir. *starts off* Laddie!

CLARENCE looks at him. McCUTCHEON speaks more gently to him.

Come on, laddie. *takes CLARENCE off* The Major's given an order.

LOUIS steps forward, pushes WALSH aside who still has his foot on SITTING BULL. LOUIS starts to help SITTING BULL up. SITTING BULL gets up by himself, LOUIS picks up SITTING BULL's blanket. SITTING BULL picks up his knife. He stands staring at WALSH. A pause. SITTING BULL replaces knife in sheaf. WALSH's hand slowly reaches out to SIT-TING BULL, as SITTING BULL slowly turns, takes his blanket and exits. WALSH's hand drops to his side. LOUIS stares at WALSH.

LOUIS:
Is dat all for me, too?

WALSH looks up at him for a moment, then slowly nods his head. LOUIS exits. Faintly we hear "Garry-owen" which builds as WALSH straightens up and walks off.

McCUTCHEON and CLARENCE march on with trunk. They drop it — Bang — As music ends. On the trunk is written: Major James Walsh, N.W.M.P. No. 7 Garden Lane, Brockville, Ontario.

CLARENCE:
I've never seen a trunk so roped up. What's he got in it?

McCUTCHEON:
When the Major says, "securely fastened", he means securely fastened.

CLARENCE:
I'd say that were excessive. You don't need that much rope, it's a waster.

McCUTCHEON:
If you want to get on in the Force, laddie, know your place. The Major decrees the tying, I oversee the tying, and you tie.

CLARENCE:
Yes, Sergeant.

McCUTCHEON:
Now get on over to the post and saddle up.

CLARENCE:
When's the Major leaving?

McCUTCHEON:
Later.

CLARENCE:
I'd like to speak to him before he goes.

McCUTCHEON:
Sorry, Constable.

CLARENCE:
I've got to see him!

WALSH approaches. They do not see him.

McCUTCHEON:
Move your ass on over to that post!

CLARENCE:
I can't go till I see him!

WALSH coughs.

McCUTCHEON:
Constable!

CLARENCE straightens to attention. WALSH glares at McCUTCHEON for not getting rid of CLARENCE, then he looks to the trunk.

WALSH:
Ah good.

CLARENCE:
Thank you, sir.

WALSH:
Bit too much rope, perhaps.

CLARENCE: *with a brief look to McCUTCHEON*
Yes sir.

WALSH: *taps one of the lashings of rope with his riding crop*
This, I think can go.

CLARENCE gets down.

CLARENCE:
Yes, sir.

WALSH:
You may go, Sergeant.   *McCUTCHEON exits.*
. . . A thing worth doing is worth doing well . . . May take more time, but that's not the point, is it?

CLARENCE:
No, sir.

WALSH:
You wanted to speak to me?

CLARENCE:
Yes, sir, I did — me and the men, a lot of us is upset, sir, about your leaving.

WALSH:
A simple leave-of-absence, Constable. I have a wife and children; it's been several years since I've seen them. Colonel MacLeod — upon my request — has kindly arranged several months off for me.

CLARENCE:
It all seemed kinda sudden.

WALSH:
I need the rest, Constable . . .   *He regrets statement — moves around the trunk.*   The lettering's not quite right. Had to have it redone. Been a long time since it's been in transit.

CLARENCE:
There's something else.

WALSH:
Yes?

CLARENCE:
It's about Sitting Bull.

WALSH:
You see a lot of him. The little boy, rather.

CLARENCE:
Yes, sir, I do. He's a very smart little boy, and I have a lot of hope for the Sioux when I talk to him, sir.

WALSH:
Do you?

CLARENCE:
Sitting Bull still considers you his friend.

WALSH:
I would have to deny that. I have my men and my wife and my children; but I have no friends. Friends are a danger. You may not comprehend that statement, Constable, but Sitting Bull would.

CLARENCE:
Maybe what I should have said was I still considered you his friend. I know you've seen me out with food and stuff, sir, and you haven't hauled me up . . . I'm not much good at sneaking.

WALSH:
That's true. I would never send you out on reconnaissance. *laughs*

CLARENCE:
No, sir.

WALSH:
What do you want to see me about, Constable?

CLARENCE:
You're goin' east to Brockville, sir. That's not too far from Ottawa. I know you've been doin' all you can from this end, but I just wondered if maybe you couldn't go up to Ottawa and tell the Prime Minister how things are. It'd make a difference. You'd make him do something.

WALSH:
Oh, yes.

CLARENCE:
Will you try and help Sittin' Bull?

WALSH:
I shall give your proposition every consideration.

McCUTCHEON:
Sorry to interrupt, sir, but . . .

WALSH:
Quite right — I must get on, Constable.

CLARENCE:
Can I tell Sittin' Bull that?

WALSH:
Our chat has been most informative, Constable. No doubt I'll see you on my return.

CLARENCE exits.

Your timing is impeccable McCutcheon.

McCUTCHEON:
I know, sir.

WALSH:
The trunk looks solid, don't you think?

McCUTCHEON:
Aye, sir.

WALSH looks after CLARENCE.

WALSH:
That young man should never make the Force his
life. *looks at McCUTCHEON and exits — as lights
dim*

*SITTING BULL enters, rolls up his buffalo robe —
looks at PRETTY PLUME and CROWFOOT. Lights
come up on HARRY who has a bottle and is singing.*

HARRY:

Oh, life in a prairie shack, when the rain begins to
pour
Drip, drip, it comes through the roof, and I want to
go home to my Ma Maw
Maw Maw I want to go home to my Maw
This bloomin' country's a fraud, and I want to go
home to my Maw.

*CLARENCE enters with cup from one direction.
LOUIS and McCUTCHEON from another.*

LOUIS:
Alors, je lui dirais, mangez la merde!

McCUTCHEON:
It's the pay, mostly, very poor pay, ye could say . . .

LOUIS:
Mangez la merde!

McCUTCHEON:
And nobody gives a damn.

CLARENCE:
Shut up! This bloody bastard's talkin' French, and you're talkin' at the same god damn time. You make me dizzy!

Everyone falls silent. They drink. Pause. Then CLARENCE speaks quietly.

Where's the Major?

LOUIS:
Eh?

McCUTCHEON:
Never mind him, Louis.

CLARENCE: *louder*
Where the hell's the god damn Major?

McCUTCHEON:
He's not here!

CLARENCE:
I know he's not here! What kind of a fool do you take me for? I know he's not here.

McCUTCHEON:
Give me another, Louis.

CLARENCE:
What kind of a leave-of-absence is 18 months? That's what I want to know.

LOUIS pours McCUTCHEON another drink. LOUIS looks at CLARENCE.

McCUTCHEON:
He's had enough. *leans towards CLARENCE* You've had enough, Clarence!

HARRY: *sings*

> This blooming country's a fraud
> And I want to go home to my Maw.

McCUTCHEON:
> Come on, y'old buzzard. Sit down and shut up!

HARRY: *coming over*

> I want to go home to my Maw.

> You boys been celebratin'?

CLARENCE:
> What?

McCUTCHEON:
> When did ye get in?

HARRY: *fills CLARENCE's cup as he enters*
> Done and over with. Signed, sealed, and delivered.
> I seen the last of Sittin' Bull!

CLARENCE:
> How'd it go?

HARRY:
> Me and 5 or 6 of the boys from C Troop, we
> escorted him down to the border with nary an
> incident – the boys signed him over, and then they
> came back up.

CLARENCE:
> Where was you?

HARRY:
> Sittin' Bull, he asked me to go on down to Fort
> Robson with him. That's where they was gonna be
> picked up and taken over to the reservation.

CLARENCE:
Yeah?

HARRY:
So I did!

CLARENCE:
Everythin' go all right?

HARRY:
You know that old horse he was ridin'? Bluecoats took that and everthin' else — said they wouldn't be needing guns or horses where they was goin'.

CLARENCE:
I never seen a Sioux without some kind of horse standin' by. *insinuating that HARRY's a liar*

HARRY:
Yeah. Well, they sure looked a sight. Real rag-tag bunch, I'm tellin' you.

Pause as they drink.

CLARENCE:
How was they takin' them to the reservation with no horses?

HARRY:
Walkin' them . . . 'cept Sittin' Bull.

CLARENCE:
What about Sittin' Bull?

HARRY:
They put him on some boat. Gonna take him down to Fort Randall.

CLARENCE:
Fort Randall.

LOUIS:
Dat's da military prison.

CLARENCE:
Why's he goin' there?

HARRY:
Why'd you think?

CLARENCE:
The agreement was nobody'd be punished. *pause*
Ain't that right?

HARRY:
I don't know nothin' 'bout what's right — all's I know
is that Sittin' Bull's in Fort Randall for killin' Custer.

CLARENCE:
What . . . what'd he do when they told him?

HARRY:
He said somethin' 'bout not goin' — not havin' to —
one of them bluecoats just give him a good clip on
the side of the head with his rifle butt and they
carried him aboard. Weren't nothin' to it. Yessireee,
I seen a historical sight — I seen the end of the Sioux
Nation.

CLARENCE:
That's not true!

HARRY:
Was you there!? . . . That boat moved off down the
river and all them Injuns lined up along the bank
makin' this terrible moanin' sound. I'm telling you it
was somethin' to see. *pause* What's the matter with
you bastards? . . . Me, Harry, is gonna propose a
toast! *holds up the bottle, LOUIS and McCUT-
CHEON hold their glasses up* Here's to the Sioux!
. . . They won the battle but they lost the war!

CLARENCE throws his drink in HARRY's face.

*HARRY stands up, throws one punch at CLAR-
ENCE which knocks him cold. McCUTCHEON,
LOUIS carry CLARENCE off, as HARRY looks at
the audience.*

Bottoms up!   *he drinks*

HARRY:

Sir John A's policy for dealin with the Sioux was an
all round winner — beats Custer all to hell. Not half
so messy as ridin' into tube-like hollows at ungodly
hours of the mornin' — and no need for a marchin'
band. Quiet, simple and effective. Do not delay in
returning to the United States, for that course is the
only alternative to death by starvation. So Sittin'
Bull left the Canadian West,   *WALSH enters, stands
behind desk.*   . . . and Major Walsh returned to it.
Yessirree, beat Custer all to hell.

*McCUTCHEON formally carries on large board, on it
a map with toy soldiers, a train engine, trees.
HARRY looks at it as McCUTCHEON places it on
the desk. HARRY laughs.*

Je-sus!   *exits, shaking his head*

WALSH:

The railway track is here — there is a slight curve
here around a grove of trees — do you see that,
McCutcheon?

McCUTCHEON:

Aye sir.

WALSH:

I think possibly 20 men could be concealed amongst
those trees — 20 men — do we have 20 men we can
rely on? Top notch fellows?

McCUTCHEON:
Aye sir.

WALSH:
Good. In an operation like this, there is no room for error. Image of the Force and all that . . . So . . . the men are concealed here. *taps map* at 2:10 precisely, the train should round this curve . . . You follow me?

McCUTCHEON:
Aye sir.

WALSH:
All right . . . Now, as the train reaches this point, Harry pulls out with a full load across the tracks . . .

McCUTCHEON:
Isn't that a bit dangerous, sir?

WALSH looks at him sharply.

I mean, sir, will the train have ample time to stop, sir?

WALSH:
All that is calculated. *coldly* Would you care to check my figures?

McCUTCHEON:
No sir, just wondering.

WALSH: *staring at him*
Good. *back to map* Now, as the train pulls up, the men, myself at the head — there'll be a dress parade before, I told you that, didn't I?

McCUTCHEON:
Aye sir.

WALSH:

Right! I will ride out from the woods, my men behind me, and all of us in full dress — tell the men to practice war whoops. I want good full-blooded Indian yells, you hear?

McCUTCHEON:

Aye sir.

WALSH:

So out we come — yelling bloody murder — I'll swing aboard the train and ride it into Calgary. Well, what do you think? Is that a stirring sight or not?

McCUTCHEON:

Very stirring, sir.

WALSH:

When you open a railroad, you do it in style, I say! Bloody train will be full of easterners and we'll scare the pants off every one of them. I want a good show.

CLARENCE: *enters, followed by LOUIS*
Major.

WALSH: *topping him*
Underhill! You have interrupted an important conference!

CLARENCE:

Beggin' your pardon, sir. Request permission to speak, sir!

WALSH: *long-suffering*
What is it?

CLARENCE:

A rider's come in from Standin' Rock. Been in the saddle all night.

WALSH:
And?

LOUIS:
. . . He's dead . . . Da white man have da Indian
Police kill 'im . . . Sittin' Bull is dead! Da rider say
he see his face bleed empty, and Death come starin'
in it's place.

CLARENCE:
They shot him twice and put the boots to him, and
Little Crow says the soldiers dropped him in a pit of
lime so's his people couldn't bury him proper.

WALSH is frozen staring at CLARENCE.

And Crowfoot . . . do you remember Crowfoot, sir?
He used to come up the fort, sir and us men, we used
to play with him 'cause he was just a kid, and ain't
none of us got kids here, and he was a real good boy.
And I liked him, sir . . . And they drug him out from
under the bed where he was hidin', and they threw
him down, and they shot him and he's dead too!
anger is spent   I come in to tell you, sir . . . 'cause
. . . 'cause . . . I didn't know what else to do.

*WALSH stands so still he seems a statue. There is a
long pause. At last WALSH speaks.*

WALSH:
Dis-missed . . .

*McCUTCHEON, CLARENCE, LOUIS make no move
to leave.*

DIS-MISSED! *They exit.*

*WALSH watches them leave. He moves to table,
looks at it. He undoes the leather holster and takes
out the gun. As he does this, we hear the sounds of
the Nez Perces from the end of ACT 1. That sound
continues as he lays the gun on the desk, and slowly
and carefully removes his tunic and puts it on the
desk. We hear SITTING BULL's voice as WALSH
slowly lifts both hands over his head.*

*SITTING BULL speaks softly, reminiscent of his
speaking to CROWFOOT, Act II.*

SITTING BULL:
In the beginning . . . was given . . . to everyone a cup.
. . . A cup of clay. And from this cup we drink our
life. We all dip in the water, but the cups are different
. . . My cup is broken. It has passed away.

WALSH slams his hands down on the desk.

BLACKOUT

116